DANCE HANDBOOK

MARGERY J. TURNER, Ed.D.

Douglass College
Rutgers—The State University
New Brunswick, New Jersey

Photography by
JOHN McCLOSKEY

12769

1959

Englewood Cliffs, N.J.
PRENTICE-HALL, INC.

J. M. HODGES LIBRARY
WHARTON COUNTY JUNIOR COLLEGE
WHARTON, TEXAS

©, 1959, BY

PRENTICE-HALL, INC.

Englewood Cliffs, N.J.

All rights reserved. No part of this book
may be reproduced in any form, by mimeo-
graph or any other means, without permission in writing from the publishers.

LIBRARY OF CONGRESS
CATALOGUE CARD No.: 59-11354

PRINTED IN THE UNITED STATES OF AMERICA

19677

12769

Preface

This book is intended to be an introductory and foundational guide for self-help in learning to do various types of dancing. It is specifically written for the layman and is therefore serviceable to general college students, as well as to church groups, clubs, agencies, and various other organizations.

The book is designed for easy reference to the various types of dance without undue reference to other parts of the book. It is also arranged to be read from cover to cover. Imaginative and resourceful readers can visibly teach themselves a great deal from this book. However, it is always a great help to have someone with whom to check accuracy of interpretation.

The purpose of this book is to provide an orientation to all forms of dance generally taught in schools today. The content is limited to the fundamental skills needed for each type of dance, with a limited number of variations, developments, or problems—whatever is applicable in each case. Because it is impossible to get both breadth and depth within the limitations of one book, each chapter is followed by selected source materials to provide further experience in each particular form of dance. The attempt is made to present clear-cut directions in simple form, without burdensome detail. In other words, this is not a complete story, but rather the begin-

J. M. HODGES LIBRARY
WHARTON COUNTY JUNIOR COLLEGE
WHARTON, TEXAS

ning of many stories. The development and endings are for the reader to determine.

I am deeply appreciative and indebted to many who assisted in the process of developing this book. I am greatly indebted to Catherine L. Allen for her constant and consistent support, help of various kinds, criticism, and work in the initial planning of the book; and to Ruth L. Samsel for her continuous interest and help in reading and criticism and for various tedious jobs of checking and typing. I am appreciative of the co-operation of my students Michael Boccio, Corinne Carrillo, and Carolyn Krawic, and of the McCloskey family—Adele, Basil, Brenden, Damian, Fabian, Justin, Mark, and Pat for their interest and co-operation in photographic illustrations, and to John McCloskey for his unending help and keen interest in producing illustrations of high quality.

I am also deeply appreciative of the permission granted for use of various materials by Barnes and Noble, Inc., The Caxton Printers, Burgess Publishing Co., the Folk Dance Federation of California, Michael Herman, Dvora Lapson of the Jewish Education Committee of New York, Fred Leifer, the Methodist Publishing House, Ronald Press, and RCA Victor.

MARGERY J. TURNER

93.3
85d

✣ *Contents*

To LLOYD SHAW . . .

> . . . Father of Square Dance
> . . . Teacher
> . . . Author and
> . . . Great American . . .

Who will continue to live through the inspiration
of those whose lives he touched.

The McCloskey Family in a Grand Right and Left.

CHAPTER I

Introduction

Dancing has been an integral part of practically every culture from ancient times to the present. It has manifested itself in a variety of forms and for a variety of purposes. It has reflected the history of peoples in a dynamic and realistic, as well as a mystical, way.

The impulse to move began with the beginnings of man, and it was only a very short time until dance was given birth as a result of this impulse. As man became more aware of the necessity for group living, his dance became a group venture reflecting his religious beliefs and social strivings. Primitive man danced about love, fear, anger, hate, and war. He imitated animals, and he danced to please the gods. As the human race grew and developed, dance became a social venture and took on more intimate group forms. As small groups banded together to become larger groups, and as larger groups banded together to become nations, dance developed to serve the evolving social and esthetic needs of man.

Throughout the history of man, in spite of unfavorable conditions, dance has survived in various forms. It flourished with primitive man, was extremely suppressed during the medieval period, was again revived during the Renaissance period, and has enjoyed a continued acceptance and upward trend of development since the Renaissance.

It is very possible that dance survives and flourishes because it affords us pleasure regardless of whether we are participators or spectators. Possibly the

1

rhythm satisfies a real need; possibly it is man's love of motion which spurs him to perpetuate dancing; possibly it is all of these and more.

In considering dance generally, we can say several things about it. Dancing, interpreted broadly as rhythmic pulse and organization of movement, probably preceded man himself; that is, dance can be found in recognizable forms in movement of life itself, as is observable in animals and birds. In its broadest sense, dance is the mother of the arts, existing in time and space simultaneously with its creator. The content of dance is life as seen through the perception of its creator. The most immediate vehicle for expression of this being is the body, which is designed for action. The body becomes an expressive vehicle through education, and the pattern for this education is set very early in life.

One need only observe the infant and the small child to see how the individual in his early life enlarges his world through movement experience: it is his way of learning. He is physically active —exploring, feeling, and observing. His responses are total body responses, and his enjoyment and frustrations are total body experiences. This total-involvement kind of learning must be kept alive. The loss of this gift of honest expression, as a child grows older, too often comes about as society and the family place restrictions upon him and cause the development of inhibitions. Although some inhibitions are necessary for adjustment and a normal life, many are thwarting and cause frustrations that impede ad-

justment and stifle spontaneity. Feelings and emotions are part of all human beings and basic to expression. The esthetic needs of man lead him to artistic expression through various media. In dance, man strives to express himself through the medium of movement.

One can also say, speaking of dance generally, that dance is a medium through which repressed powers are given freedom, motion, and a sensed order. The dancer loses himself in movement with its exhilarating effects. He travels through time, space, and psychological barriers. Dance gives vent to imagination, fancy, and creativity in general. Through dance man is able to rise above the earthly world and sense newfound power. In discussing this point, Curt Sachs says, "The dance, inherited from savage ancestors as an ordered expression in motion of the exhilaration of the soul, develops and broadens into the search for God, into the conscious effort to become a part of those powers beyond the might of man which control our destinies. The dance becomes a sacrificial rite, a charm, a prayer, and a prophetic vision. It summons and dispels the forces of nature, heals the sick, links the dead to the charm of their descendants; it assures sustenance, luck in chase, victory in battle; it blesses the fields and the tribe. It is creator, preserver, steward and guardian." [1]

Dance has served as religious experience for many of our great artists. Ruth St. Denis has probably been the best-known exponent of religious dance of our time. It is not uncommon to find that

---

[1] Curt Sachs, *World History of Dance* (New York: W. W. Norton and Company, 1937), p. 4.

many artists' religious concepts have been developed through the medium of their art. Probably the greatest influence controlling the rise and fall of dancing through the centuries has been that of religion. From the earliest times, dancing was an important part of religious ceremonies—much of which was displayed as religious fanaticism. St. Johnston states, "Religious fanaticism fills men with a sudden rush of frenzied thought and incoherent ideas, and as a result calm and intelligent reason is swept aside and control over body action is lost. And to work off this superfluous energy strong muscular action takes place. So probably were the religious dances, produced by a constant dwelling on religious ideas. These dances, once inaugurated, became more organized and methodical until they took their place among regular ceremonial observances of each particular religion. Dance could express so much that was necessary in the act of worship, thanksgiving, praise, supplication and humiliation, it is not surprising it became an important factor in the history of religion. The one idea running through all religious dances from early times is to attract attention of the deity by violent exertions, and to force the notice of their needs upon him by the vigour of their dancing." [2] It is upon this concept of the purpose served by dance that we base many of our convictions concerning psychotherapy through dancing. While such study is very much in its infancy, it promises to be a channel for working out problems, reviving the ability to communicate, and releasing tension through physical and emotional channels. Such therapy is undeveloped at present because of the need for the combined efforts of highly specialized people in dance, clinical psychology, and medicine. The foundation skills are yet to be developed. There is not much question that dance did serve a therapeutic function in the lives of primitive societies. This point is further delineated by Urlin's discussion of primitive dances, in which she states, "The Maoris have a scalp dance, as do the Red Indians; the Sudanese dance to celebrate victories over their enemies; the Dakota Indians paint themselves black and sing and dance war dirges to pacify the souls of those slain in battle; the wives of warriors who have left home for the field of battle perform day and night ceremonial dances to keep up the courage of their husbands; a dance of death is known among all savage tribes on the principle of like counteracting like; exorcism of evil spirits is effected by the same means through devil and ghost dances and for healing diseases." [3] Urlin believes that the origin of dance is based on a blend of three principles:

1. Ceremonial or religious dancing, imitative of movement spheres, as they were called in the ancient cosmogony.
2. Dramatic or histrionic representa-

---

[2] Reginald St. Johnston, *A History of Dancing* (London: Simpkin, Marshall, Hamilton and Kent Co., 1906), pp. 17-19.

[3] Ethel L. H. Urlin, *Dancing, Ancient and Modern* (New York: Appleton-Century-Crofts Co., 1914), p. 3.

tions of man's chief passions—love and war.

3. Mimicry of animals, as an outcome of the belief in animal ancestry.

Dancing played a larger part in the everyday life of the primitive than it does in our culture primarily because it was easier to express ideas by gesture than by speech. Since appreciation of rhythm and musical sound is a fundamental principle of man's nature, it is natural to find it bound up with the primitive races of mankind.

Dancing has always incorporated the element of play as part of its activity. The value of play has only recently come into its own and been appreciated as a sound method of education as well as therapy. Huizinga, in his excellent book on theory of play says, "Play is older than culture, for culture, however inadequately defined, always presupposes human society, and animals have not waited for man to teach them playing."[4] In discussing the principle of play in relation to archaic culture, he states, "The sacred performance is more than an actualization in appearance only, a sham reality; it is also more than a symbolical actualization—it is a mystical one. In it something invisible and inactual takes beautiful, actual and holy form. The participants in the rite are convinced that the action actualizes and effects a definite beatification, brings about an order of things higher than that in which they customarily live. All the same this actualization by representation still retains

the formal characteristics of play in every respect. It is played or performed within a playground that is literally staked out and played moreover as a feast, i.e., in mirth and freedom."[5]

The historical backgrounds of the forms of dance which we know best today are varied, owing to religious and cultural differences of people of various races and national origins. By and large, all forms of dance we know and practice today incorporate the play element and are done primarily for socialization and recreation, with the exception of forms such as ballet and modern dance. These forms, on the concert stage, are practiced primarily for the sake of art. Off stage they are used for many other purposes. We still find the fanatics in dance, whether religious or non-religious. We still see the symbolic dances of the Greeks, Jews, Poles, and Scandinavians danced at weddings, christenings, and other festival events. If we go to the Southwest, we can still see the snake, fertility, and other ceremonial dances of the American Indians. In the areas where Christianity has been imposed on the Indians, we find that they still prefer their own rituals, gods, and medicine men although they have accepted Christianity, at least in part. Rhythm, the ongoing pulse of movement, is evident in all groups. Rhythmic flow and motion in worship is still a strong cultural pattern of the southern Negroes, as is their love of jazz which is done with real abandon and exhilaration. Dance as an integral part of life is most clearly

---

[4] Johan Huizinga, *Homo Ludens, A Study of the Play Element in Culture*, p. 4.
[5] *Ibid.*, p. 4.

exemplified in the American Indian and Negro.

The impulse to dance is the impulse to live. We are biological structures designed for movement. We move in a universal rhythm and derive satisfaction from it. We are living in an era of dynamic changes linked to the past with equally dynamic impulses, and our music and dance reflect the changes taking place. The movement in our dances today personifies the generation we live in, and this will be true tomorrow, too, when today will have become yesterday.

And so dancing was born with the earliest human societies. It has been identified with various forms of worship and has progressed and developed with them. Dancing has been an integral part of the lives of all peoples, has depicted their customs and religious yearnings, has survived through centuries of change, and lives today. Dancing, like all human institutions, is one of action and reaction. It makes its entrance, has its periods of development and decline, but continues to exist and spring forth with new, robust beginnings.

CHAPTER II

Foundations for Good Dancing

LOOKING ALIVE

Have you ever looked in a full-length mirror when you felt happy? Have you ever imagined that you looked like your favorite movie star? Have you ever seen yourself in a movie that you didn't know was being taken? These are very important and valuable experiences, but sometimes they are hard to take. Maybe this discussion will help you find ways of looking the way you would like to see yourself. As Margaret H'Doubler so aptly said to many of her classes, "Good dancing is not concerned with a beautiful body moving, but rather with a body moving beautifully." If it is "what you do with what you've got" that is im-

portant, we can all learn to move beautifully.

Moving beautifully depends a great deal on how you carry your body. First, you must desire to stand with the grace and stature of royalty—outgoing, and proud to be alive. There isn't any advantage in ambling about with that ever-so-common "excuse me for living" attitude. If you cannot find any good reason for standing elegantly, try it anyway, and see if you don't feel like a different person.

The easiest way to look like the illustration on the next page is to stretch your body as high as possible, making your profile as thin as possible. Relax the shoulders, tilt the chest upward, stretch the neck, hold the chin high, and center the weight over the balls of the feet.

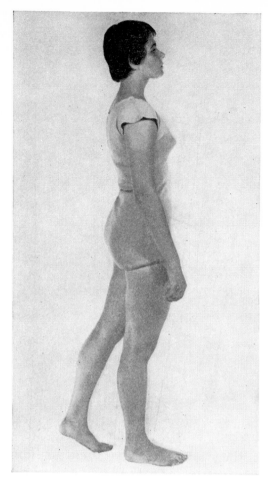

Carriage of the Body.

MOVING WITH MOTIVATION

Now that you are in your best posture, start walking. Do you walk with a purpose, or do you appear uninterested in where you are going? If you will imagine you are going to meet a dear friend or someone you really want to see, you may be motivated to walk with a purpose. The directness of moving is usually a result of having a reason for going. You will look most alive when you walk with

a purpose. With practice, you will develop a habit of standing and walking in good posture. Eventually, you will enjoy looking and feeling alive because it makes you feel good. This will happen when you become aware of how you feel when you move.

AWARENESS

Have you ever noticed how your friends move when they are happy? How do their movements and posture change when they have disappointments and frustrations? We are creatures who have feelings, and we generally express these feelings unconsciously through our bodies, thus sharing these feelings with others. Becoming aware of these feelings and of the ways our bodies express those feelings is necessary before we can find and experience relationships between movement and meaning. The body is capable of saying many things through movement that cannot be said adequately in words. Movement is the medium through which we express ourselves in dancing. As we become more sensitive and aware, we develop greater depth for expressing ourselves as well as for understanding the expressions of others. The more aware we are of our expressive habits, the better position we are in to use them effectively or to discard them for new ones. This awareness is not only intellectual and emotional, but kinesthetic * as well. As our muscles get in tune, we find ourselves better equipped to execute controlled movement as we feel it.

* See the Glossary.

BEING ALIVE

When we become sensitive to movement and feeling, our bodies become alive. Everyone has experienced this feeling at some time in life. It is observable in a child who, at play, is completely involved in an enjoyable learning experience. This feeling is also observed in the performance of an expert diver, or in a beautiful performance in any activity. What is observable is total involvement, motivation, and searching or problem-solving behavior. The thrill of feeling alive is the fountain of youth. Once it is attained, it can be sustained. To achieve this quality of being, perseverance and practice, as well as a strong desire to be a vital person, are required.

FEELING THE WORLD AROUND US

Space Awareness: Are you aware of how it feels to stand on a mountain and look down into a canyon? Can you imagine how it feels to go through a tunnel and come out into open space? Do you imagine it feels different to be a spectator in a theater watching those on stage from the way it feels to be the performer on stage looking at the audience? If you think back, you will undoubtedly recall experiences you have had that are similar to these. These differences in feeling are the result of our awareness of the world around us. It is essentially space awareness. Space has many forms, shapes, and even textures. Space has a very definite effect on our feelings as well as on our movement.

We travel uptown, downtown, and across town through space. We identify this traveling as going in a particular direction. There are many directions we can go, but, by and large, we go forward and backward, sideward right and left, diagonally forward and backward right and left, up, down, and around in circles. These directions are shown in the illustration below:

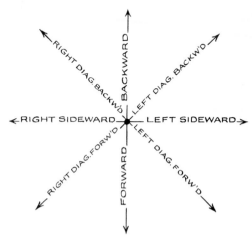

Figure 1. Directions.

We may travel on the ground level by bus, above the ground level by elevated trains, and below the ground level by subway. These are levels, and, although there are many levels between these, we generally organize our thoughts about level in terms of major divisions, of degrees known as high, medium, and low. In our travels, we find certain experiences are more interesting than others, and we focus greater attention on them. Direction in space, level, and focus are also factors of body movement. When you become aware of these factors and use them consciously, you will become space-conscious.

If you are going to be one of the

"bodies moving beautifully," being aware of the world around you is a *must*. This awareness will help you move through space feeling a part of it, regardless of the type of dancing you are performing. It will help you make conscious use of direction in moving. It will make you conscious of using a variety of levels and help you to define your movement by pinpointing the focus of it. These elements of space, direction, level, and focus belong to all types of dancing. Through the awareness and conscious use of these elements, your movement will become alive and interesting and you will derive increased pleasure from your accomplishment.

Traveling Through Space: Let us start with your very best posture and run in a forward direction through space. Remember, you are to run as though you wanted to get there. Go directly, pressing forward with your whole body. If you are going to do this efficiently, you must go "in one piece." In order to do this, shift your weight forward in a straight line from the ankles to the head. Lean far enough forward so that you have to run to keep your body from falling. This brings up the subject of elevating the body to levels higher than standing. While elevation is not a great problem in running, the principle of elevation—namely, that of constantly defying gravity—is a part of all movement. Whether you walk, run, leap, hop, or jump, the principle of working against gravity is the same. It involves:

LEG AND FOOT ACTION:

On leaving the floor, the push-away happens as a result of using the buttocks muscles, the calf of the leg, and the foot and toes in pressing against the floor. On landing, the toes reach the floor first, followed by the heel, the bending of the knee, and tightening of the thigh and buttocks—all of which will produce a light landing. This action is illustrated in the photograph on the next page.

BODY ACTION:

The body must be ready to go up and have enough tension to hold it solid without being rigid. Think high, feel light, and act as though gravity were no problem at all.

This method of defying gravity applies whether you transfer your weight from one foot to the other or whether it returns to the same foot. It also applies to a less visible degree in walking. However, visible or invisible, no matter what you do, you are resisting gravity and aiming at a suspension of the body giving a feeling of lightness.

What are the fundamental ways that you can travel through space? There are five. You may travel through space by:

WALKING

Transfer the weight from one foot to the other; one foot is in contact with the floor as the other foot swings forward.

RUNNING

Use the same action as a walk but do it much faster. In a run, there is a moment when both feet are off the floor at the same time.

HOPPING

Push off from one foot and land on the same foot, or push off from two feet and land on one foot.

JUMPING

Push off from two feet, go into the air, and land on two feet.

LEAPING

Push off from one foot, go into the air, and land on the other foot. A leap is higher than a run.

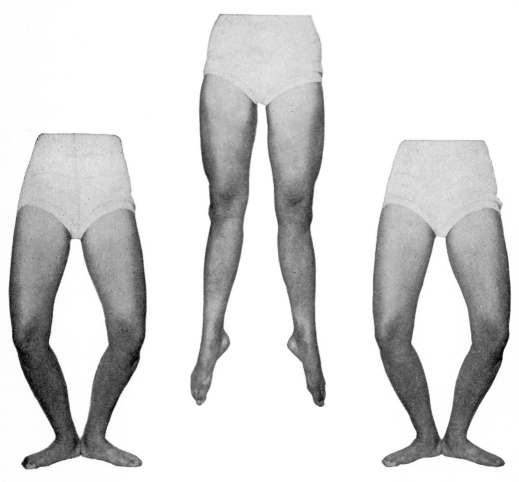

Elevation of the Body: (a) preparing, (b) pushing away, (c) landing.

All other basic ways of traveling are derived from these five fundamental ways of moving through space.

The following steps are basic to many forms of dancing. It will be to your advantage to learn them well, as they will aid you in gaining skill more rapidly.

SKIP

Consists of a step and a hop in uneven rhythm. Push off the floor on the step, going high into the air, and land on the same foot. The push-off is longer than the landing. The step pattern is step-hop. Two skips are completed to one measure.

GALLOP

Consists of a step and a leap. The push-off from the step is longer than the landing on the leap. The step pattern is step-leap. Two gallops are completed to one measure.

SLIDE

Consists of a sliding step and a close, shifting the weight on the close. The slide is longer than the close. The step pattern is slide-close. Two slides are completed to a measure.

TWO-STEP

Consists of a step forward or sideward, a close with the other foot, a step forward or sideward again, and a pause. One two-step is completed to a measure. The step pattern is step-close-step-hold.

WALTZ

Consists of three steps, bringing the feet together on the third step. The first step is always either forward or backward, the second step is sideward or diagonal, and the third step is always a close. Each step is of equal time duration. The step pattern is step-step-close. One waltz step is completed to a measure.

SCHOTTISCHE

Consists of three steps and a hop, generally taken forward. Each step is of equal time duration. One schottische step is completed to a measure. The step pattern is step-step-step-hop.

POLKA

Consists of three steps and a hop. The polka rhythm is uneven; that is, each step does not get the same amount of time. The third step is given a longer time than the first and second steps. One polka step is completed to a measure. The step pattern is step-step-step-hop.

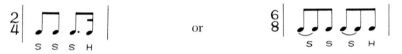

MAZURKA

Consists of a step diagonally forward left with the left foot, a close with the right foot (at the same time kick the left foot diagonally forward), a hop on the right foot (as you bring the left foot across the right ankle). Each step is of equal time duration, but the second step is accented. One Mazurka is completed to a measure. The step pattern is step-close-hop.

SELECTED READING

General Reading and Reference Material

Beaumont, Cyril W., *A Bibliography of Dancing*. London: The Dancing Times Ltd., 1929.

Boas, Franziska, *The Function of Dance in Human Society: A Seminar Directed by F. Boas*. New York: The Boas School, 1944.

Bouchard, Thomas, "The Preservation of the Dance Score Through Filming the Dance," in Sorrell, Walter, *The Dance Has Many Faces*. Cleveland: World Publishing Company, 1951.

Bowers, Faubion, *The Dance in India*. New York: Columbia University Press, 1953.

Broom, Leonard, and Frank G. Speck, *Cherokee Dance and Drama*. Berkeley: University of California Press, 1951.

Chujoy, Anatole (ed.), *The Dance Encyclopedia*. New York: Ronald Press, 1949.

Dewey, John, *Art as Experience*. New York: Minton, Balch and Company, 1934.

Espinosa, Edouard A., *The Complete Technical Dictionary of Dancing*. London: The Dancer, 1935.

Gorer, Geoffrey, *Africa Dances: A Book About West African Negroes*. London: Faber and Faber, 1935.

Henius, Frank (arr.), *Songs and Games of the Americas*. New York: Scribner, 1943.

Kelley, Earl C., *Education for What Is Real*. New York: Harper and Bros., 1947.

Lane, Janet, *Your Carriage, Madam: A Guide to Good Posture*. New York: John Wiley and Sons, Inc., 1947.

Mearns, Hugh, *The Creative Adult*. New York: Doubleday, Doran and Co., 1940.

O'Moor, Mary (ed.), *ABC's of Dance Terminology*. Washington, D.C.: Dance Masters of America, Inc., 1949.

Sachs, Curt, *The Commonwealth of Art: Style in the Fine Arts, Music and Dance*. New York: Norton, 1946.

Sorrell, Walter (ed.), *The Dance has Many Faces*. Cleveland: World Publishing Company, 1951.

Wessel, Janet A., *Movement Fundamentals, Figure, Form, Fun*. New York: Prentice-Hall, Inc., 1957.

History of Dance

Chalif, Louis H., *Folk Dances of Different Nations*. New York: Louis H. Chalif, 1926.

Dannett, Sylvia G., and Frank R. Rachel, *Down Memory Lane*. New York: Greenberg, 1954. (Arthur Murray's picture story of dancing.)

Haskell, Arnold L., *Dancing Around the World*. New York: Dodge, 1938.

Hofer, Mari Ruef, *Polite and Social Dances: A collection of historic dances, Spanish, Italian, French, German, American*. Chicago: Clayton F. Summy Co., 1917.

Kinney, Troy and Margaret, *The Dance*. New York: Frederick A. Stokes Co., 1924.

Kirstein, Lincoln E., *Dance*. New York: G. P. Putnam's Sons, 1935.

Magriel, Paul D., *Chronicles of the American Dance*. New York: Holt, 1948.

Marks, Joseph E., *America Learns to Dance: A Historical Study of Dance Ed-ucation in America Before 1900*. New York: Exposition Press, 1957.

Moore, Lillian, *Artists of the Dance*. New York: Cromwell, 1938.

Pischl, A. J., *A Catalogue of Souvenir Dance Programs*. New York: Dance Index, 1948.

Sachs, Curt. *World History of the Dance* (translated by Bessie Schoenberg). New York: W. W. Norton and Co., 1937.

Sharp, Cecil, and A. P. Oppé, *The Dance: An Historical Survey of Dancing in Europe*. London: Halton and Truscott Smith Ltd., 1924.

Urlin, Ethel, L.H., *Dancing, Ancient and Modern*. New York: Appleton-Century-Crofts, 1914.

Vuillier, Gaston, *A History of Dancing from the Earliest Ages to Our Own Times*. New York: Appleton-Century-Crofts, 1898.

CHAPTER III

Modern Dance

Modern, or contemporary, dance is a type of dance that uses the body as a means of expressing feelings, ideas, emotions, moods, or situations. There are many principles that govern the creative side of modern dance, and the composer or choreographer adheres to certain principles when he or she creates a dance.

Before we get into creating dance, however, let's begin at the beginning and talk about movement, since dance is movement. Movement, of course, can be a general term, but here the term specifically refers to expressive movement that communicates meaning to others. Let's start at the very beginning and consider the instrument with which we have to work.

We have the human body as our instrument of expression and movement as the medium through which expression is achieved. Expressive movement is dependent on what we do with the instrument, and the instrument, in turn, is dependent on body structure. Structurally, the human body is designed for certain fundamental ways of moving. These ways are known to you as bending and stretching, twisting and turning, rising and falling.* These are basic movements that can be done in an endless number of ways. These movements are essentially total body movements and can be

---

* See the Glossary.

done in place or while traveling from one place to another.

Movement that travels from one place to another is called *locomotor* * movement. The fundamental ways we travel through space are by walking, running, leaping, jumping, hopping, skipping, and galloping. These are specific co-ordinations of the feet and legs (see pages 9-10). These different ways of moving that we call fundamental are the foundations for all the variation of movement that we use in modern dance.

Up to this point we have been concerned with movement itself—the basis for all activities. Now we must think in terms of how movement becomes meaningful, or how it can express feeling and communicate to others. To achieve communication, movement needs motivation. This implies not only a definite intention on your part but also an awareness of your body in relation to the time (rhythmic) and space factors that give movement a live existence. For example, a walk and a twist can show impatience, but they can also show escape, search, and many other feeling states, depending on your intention and the particular use you make of rhythmic and spatial factors. The tempo you choose, the degree of tension, your focus or concentration, the movement itself, the rhythmic pattern it takes, the amount of space you use, the way you use it, and many other factors contribute to the resultant communication. Because variation is so infinite, sharpening your sensitivity to movement is important. For

best results, know what you want to achieve and develop your own method of solving the problem, evaluating what you are doing as you compose as well as evaluating when you have finished a study. Once you tackle a problem, stick to it until you have completed it. Avoid the error of changing the problem as you meet barriers; these are the experiences that produce growth, if you see them through, and you will learn a great deal from them. One word of caution here: do not expect every movement to have a specific meaning. The only time each movement has a specific meaning is in pantomime and gesture, both of which are highly mimetic.

To motivate movement implies the use of imagination. Probably the greatest resource we have for developing the imagination, as well as for developing spontaneity, is the practice of improvisation—the act of composing on the spur of the moment. Improvisation is a spontaneous response to some stimulus. In this case, it is response in the form of movement. In solving movement problems, you may use a number of different stimuli * to get the response that answers the problem. Many different stimuli are used for dance improvisation, such as music, words, rhythm, objects of varying kinds, and even movement itself. Anything that stimulates the individual through one or more of the six senses (sight, taste, tactile, hearing, smell, and kinesthetic *) may be used as a stimulus. For a fuller discussion of improvisation, see the author's book

---

* See the Glossary.

Improvisation.

Modern Dance for High School and College.[1]

Now that we've considered the ways in which the body can move and how ideas and movement can be related, let's consider the subject of dance composition or choreography. Beginners who attend a modern dance program may not understand the dances they see. This is understandable because there are many different approaches to dance, and the beginner is quite unaware of this fact. In fact, some dancers have become

so highly stylized and individualistic in their performance that few people do understand what they are doing.

The following diagram shows one way of organizing the concept of dance composition into an understandable form. There are various kinds of dance composition, and each must be observed with certain limitations. Think of the various types of composition as belonging to one continuum ranging in degree from the very realistic at one end to the very abstract at the other.

---

[1] Margery Turner, *Modern Dance for High School and College.* Englewood Cliffs, N.J.: Prentice-Hall, Inc., 1957, pp. 94-118.

| REALISTIC | | | | ABSTRACT |
| PANTOMIME | GESTURE | DRAMATIC CHARACTER | MOODS | PURE DANCE |

Figure 2. Classification of Dance Compositions.

Below is a brief explanation of the above classification applied to dance compositions that you are likely to see in attending a dance program.

Pantomime: Movement that is descriptive of the actions of people in specific situations. All details are considered, but the most important ones are emphasized. Pantomime is the most realistic form of movement expression. It mimics the expression of a person in a specific situation. It can be abstracted to varying degrees, but its specific meaning remains recognizable.

Gesture: A movement symbol which carries a specific meaning. It may be a movement of any one or several parts of the body, and this movement is recognizable in terms of a specific meaning (for example, waving goodbye or beckoning someone to come). Gesture, although it is realistic, can be abstracted and become more subtle in meaning than pantomime. The use of folk songs as content for dance utilizes gesture in both a pure and an abstract form.

Dramatic: A sequence of events carried by the emotional dynamics of a situation. The events themselves are important only as they are reflected in the lives of people. This also includes characterization of people, but in a form considerably more abstract than pantomime or gesture. Characterization here is based on the essence of the individual or the common denominators that make him what he is. Dramatic composition is concerned with deeper values of the individual and not with descriptive actions. Main issues are dealt with rather than specific detail.

Moods: These include stylized dances as well as dances based primarily on feeling states. In dances based on feeling or emotional states, the dancer must define her feelings very thoroughly and use this as a stimulus for creating movement that expresses this feeling. Such composition follows the dynamics of the emotional experience. It is abstract in the sense that movement is a direct response to feeling and not related to a series or sequence of events. Included also in this group are compositions that make use of symbolism, that is, that use objects as representative of meaning to which the dancer refers, reacts, and interacts.

Pure Dance: This is the extreme of abstraction, in which the thematic roots of the dance are in pure movement. Pure dance exists as a response to motor imagery.° It does not borrow or lean upon music, words, drama, realism, or any other vehicle of expression. Communication takes place in motor or kinesthetic reaction, and it is impossible to describe or translate into words the experience you get from seeing or doing pure dance composition.

° See the Glossary.

There are many variations of these classifications, just as there are many instances where one type may be mixed or fused with another, and sometimes it is hard to separate them or draw the line between one type and another. This classification is merely a guidepost to help you understand the differences you may see. Actually, the best prescription for viewing dance is to be completely open-minded to what you see and to allow yourself to be moved by the dance as you watch. After it is over, you should make an attempt at organizing your reactions. Do not go hunting for what you are led to expect by the title of the dance, and try not to read into it the meaning you want to give it. Be patient with the abstract dances—you have to look at them a while before you begin to appreciate or develop any feeling for them. Pantomime is enjoyable, and the way some people do it makes it an art. It is very easy to understand. Try to formulate your own questions and answers and develop a concept of dance from your own experience. This will take a few years, but it is an enjoyable leisure pursuit.

What are the minimum essentials that should be included in a dance composition? An effective dance composition should have a beginning, middle, and end. It should embody an order that is logical or coherent with the content that the dancer is expressing. Movement should follow a natural course of development, with one movement growing out of another. A composition should embody the following structures in some form: movement, emotion, rhythm, space, and design.[2]

Following is a list of problems for you to solve. They include all types and are designed to help you (a) become more inventive in creating movement that communicates, (b) become aware of the various parts of your body and discover new ways of using them, (c) experience a variety of ways of moving as a foundation for further creative experience. You will notice that there is little use of music suggested. This is done so that you will become more aware of movement and of your own natural rhythm. After you have worked through these problems, you should be ready and desirous of tackling a short dance composition.

MOVEMENT PROBLEMS

1. Go back to pages 9-10 and practice all of the basic locomotor movements until you know what they are and can perform them easily.
2. Create ten completely different movements that you have not done before; one movement should flow into the next without a break as you change from one position to another. Try to eliminate any repetition of either a total or a partial movement.

---

[2] Margery Turner, *Modern Dance for High School and College*. Englewood Cliffs, N.J.: Prentice-Hall, Inc., 1957, p. 150.

3. Create a phrase of movement that includes the following: (a) travel from one end of the room to the other; (b) two types of locomotor steps; (c) movement on three levels; (d) arm movement at some time; (e) movement continuing for at least eight counts; (f) movement based on a specific feeling or emotional quality.

4. Create a phrase of movement that uses three of the following movement qualities: percussive, sustained, vibratory, swinging, collapsing.*

5. Dance your interpretation of the feelings expressed in the following telegrams:

   (a) Best wishes to the newlyweds, smiles, cheer, and sunshine galore!
   (b) May you get the wishbone of the turkey, and may all of your Thanksgiving wishes come true.
   (c) Greetings from a wanderer whose feet would like relaxation under your table this day.
   (d) Another year, another candle, and a million wishes from us for the happiest of birthdays!
   (e) Thrilled and happy to hear the good news! May the new addition prove a source of joy to you always.
   (f) Blow out the candles, cut a piece of cake, wish I could be with you, helping celebrate! Happy Birthday.

6. Take a length of rope about a yard long and wind the ends around your hands until the rope is taut when the arms are stretched. Keep a steady pull on the rope as you explore different arm movements. Allow the body to change positions as the arms are moved, and then explore leg movements with arm movement. This also may be used with couples or small groups. In this event, partners must change movement in relation to each other and maintain a balance of tension on the rope. Everyone should move. The rope may be shortened or lengthened. After you have worked out a phrase you like, see if you can do it the same way without the aid of the rope to give you tension and balance.

7. Create a mood (such as sad, glad, lackadaisical, silly, and so forth) through attitude and posture. Move the way you feel, improvising until you have a phrase that is a clear statement of your feeling. Show it to someone and see whether their interpretation is what you intended. Take the phrase and consider it as a theme. Develop it into a theme * and variation * or into a situation that has a sequence of events.

8. Choose an object in the room and concentrate your focus on it. Improvise movement and travel anywhere you wish; regardless of what you do, keep your attention and focus on this object.

9. Gestures are movements that have specific meanings, such as to wave goodbye, to beckon someone to come, to embrace, to thumb a ride, and so forth. There are many gestures. Take one and do it with a definite intention. Vary this one gesture in as many ways as possible. Each variation can give a

---

* See the Glossary.

subtle change in meaning or can reinforce the original intention. You can vary movement by changing one or more of the following: the rhythm, the size (by making the movement either smaller or larger), and the degree of tension. You may also vary a movement by doing the movement with another part of the body, by adding a supporting movement to the gesture, or by adding locomotion. Experiment with variation; but remember, the variation must be related closely enough to the gesture to be recognizable.

10. Confine yourself to one spot and indicate the following directions through movement on three levels: forward, backward, sideward (right and left), diagonally (forward and backward, right and left), up, down, and around (see page 8). Use variety in your movement and make each movement flow into the next. Sense each direction in space with your whole body.

11. Choose one of the following space forms and create it through the kind of movement that you do. In order to solve this problem, you must imagine that the space form sets actual limitations on your movement. It is one thing to crawl through a tunnel, and another thing to create the illusion of crawling through a tunnel. Imagine moving in one of the following situations: (a) long narrow passageway too narrow to turn around; (b) funnel shape—narrow at bottom to wide at top; (c) tall cylindrical shape, diameter about three feet; (d) on a cliff over a deep canyon; (e) on top of a mountain; (f) a right-triangular space in which the only place you can stand upright is on the right-angle end. Your job is to dramatize this space. You will need to improvise in exploring the problem before you decide on *how* you will solve it. During this exploration you will find ideas for content or dramatization.

12. We refer to dynamics in dance as *contrast*. You may contrast rhythms—slow rhythms with fast rhythms of varying degrees of tempo; light movement with heavy; smooth movement with sharp; large movement with small; straight movement with curved; and so forth. Start by doing a definite movement of four counts. Find a movement to contrast with it. Analyze what you have in contrasts. Work out as many contrasts as you can by improvising and/or planning. Take these movements and try to do them at the same time rather than one after the other. Some will work and some will have to be adapted.

13. Develop a movement phrase that travels on a walking base at a slow tempo. Repeat this phrase twice as fast. Do it with a partner, one taking the slow tempo and the other the fast. If you are accurate, rhythmically keeping a steady basic beat, you will finish at the same time as the person who does the fast phrase and completes it twice.

14. Take a Calypso song and find the basic beat. Move to this beat. Listen to the music for the syncopation.* Move to the syncopated pattern. Develop a sequence including torso, arm, and leg movements. At times accent a movement and hold or pause, still keeping the beat alive somewhere in the body.

---

* See the Glossary.

15. Create a sixteen-measure sequence of movement that is continuous. Adapt that sequence to one or more of the following styles: (a) ballroom, as in waltz, tango, mambo, cha cha cha, or the like; (b) country dance, as in square dance or folk dance of other countries; (c) jazz, as in rock and roll, jitterbug, or blues; (d) balletic; (e) distorted.

During the process of solving these problems, questions will undoubtedly arise concerning the performance or technical aspect of movement. Movement is technically good when it is complete. Giving movement adequate time, muscular tension, motivation, and rhythmical organization will tend to improve it technically. Balance and postural control and proper shifting of weight are essential to a polished performance. Probably the greatest factor is fulfilling your intention of the movement you create. It is beyond the intention of this book to go into the analysis of technique. However, you may find it in one of the many valuable sources that follow this chapter.

SELECTED MUSIC FOR MODERN DANCE

Records

Folkways Album #51. *Dance-A-Long* (78 RPM or LP 33⅓). Music for rhythmic exercises, dance improvisation, Waltz, Schottische, Polka, Mazurka.

Sarah Malament, *Improvisations for Modern Dance* (LP 33⅓). Sarah Malament, 3215 Wetherland Ave., New York 63, N.Y.

Freda Miller Albums (78 RPM). *Accompaniment for Dance Technique I; Second and Third Albums for Dance;* and Album IV, *Music for Rhythms and Dance.* 237 East 81st Street, New York 28, N.Y.

Piano Music

Antheil, George, *Suite for the Piano.* G. Schirmer, Inc., N.Y.

Bartok, Bela, *Mikrokosmos*, Vols. I and II. Boosey and Hawkes.

Bowles, Paul, *Six Preludes for Piano.* Music Press, Inc.

George, Earl, *Three Rounds for Piano.* Carl Fischer, Inc.

Green, Ray, *Dance Theme and Variations.* Mercury Music Corp.

Johnson, Hunter, *Piano Sonata.* Music Press, Inc.

Lobos, Villa, *Five Pieces for Piano.*

McDonald, Harl, *Two Sketches for Piano.* Elkan Vogel Co., Philadelphia.

Miller, Freda, *Accompaniment for Dance Technique.* 237 E. 81st St., New York 28, N.Y.

Thompson, Virgil, *Ten Etudes for Piano.* Carl Fischer, Inc.

SELECTED READINGS FOR MODERN DANCE

Armitage, Merle, *Martha Graham.* Los Angeles: Lynton R. Kistler Company, 1937.

Hawkins, Alma, *Modern Dance in Higher Education.* New York: Teachers College, Columbia University, 1954.

Hayes, Elizabeth, *Dance Composition and Production for High Schools and Colleges.* New York: Ronald Press, 1955.

H'Doubler, Margaret Newell, *Dance: A Creative Art Experience.* New York: Appleton-Century-Crofts, 1940.

Horst, Louis, *Pre-Classic Dance Forms.* New York: Kamin Dance Publishers, 1953.

Jones, Ruth Whitney, and Margaret De Haahn, *Modern Dance in Education.* New York: Teachers College, Columbia University, 1948.

Laban, Rudolf Von, *Modern Educational Dance.* London: MacDonald and Evans, 1948.

La Meri, *Dance as an Art Form; Its History and Development.* New York: Ronald Press, 1933.

Lloyd, Margaret, *The Borzoi Book of Modern Dance.* New York: Knopf, 1949.

Love, Paul Van Derveer, *Modern Dance Terminology.* New York: Kamin Dance Publishers, 1953.

Martin, John J., *America Dancing.* New York: Dodge Publishing Company, 1936.

————, *Introduction to the Dance.* New York: Norton, 1939.

————, *The Dance.* New York: Tudor Publishing Co., 1946.

Radir, Ruth A., *Modern Dance for the Youth of America.* New York: Ronald Press, 1944.

Selden, Elizabeth, *The Dancer's Quest; Essays.* Berkeley, California: University of California Press, 1935.

Spiesman, Mildred, *Creative Dance in American Life and Education.* Unpublished doctoral dissertation. New York: Teachers College, Columbia University, 1949.

Stewart, Virginia, *Modern Dance.* New York: E. Weyhe, 1935.

Terry, Walter, *Invitation to Dance.* New York: Barnes and Noble, Inc., 1942.

Turner, Margery J., *Modern Dance for High School and College,* Englewood Cliffs, N.J.: Prentice-Hall, Inc., 1957.

Winearls, Jane, *Modern Dance: The Jooss-Leeder Method.* London: Adam and Charles Black, 1958.

CHAPTER IV

Social Dance

Social dancing is as simple as walking, provided that you know where you want to go. In other words, all you really need to know is the direction of travel and the step pattern to be used. The variety of steps included in this chapter may seem to be a big order; but, as you learn these steps, you will note the similarities between them, and you will realize that they are all part of the same thing. After all, you can only move in so many directions in so many positions with a partner. These factors remain fairly consistent. It is the rhythmic pattern of the step and the quality of movement that change from one type of dance step to another. Remember this as you learn the steps. You will find learning more fun, you will have a better understanding of the steps,

and ultimately you will find it easier to create your own combinations.

If you want to dance well and maintain an attractive appearance while dancing, you must have proper body alignment or posture. It is necessary at all times to hold your own weight and not to shift the burden to your partner. When you maintain a lifted, upright position, your movement becomes light and easy. You are also in a better position to correct errors spontaneously, as well as to lead and/or follow.

It is important for men and women to learn to take both the "lead" and the "follow" positions in social dancing. Fitting into your partner's shoes will be a rewarding experience in terms of patience and understanding of your partner's difficulties.

J. M. HODGES LIBRARY
WHARTON COUNTY JUNIOR COLLEGE
WHARTON, TEXAS

LEADING

To lead well, you must first be sure of the steps that you are dancing; second, you must know in what direction you want to go; third, you must give clear indication of your intention to your partner in a subtle way. Do not expect your partner to be psychic—it will only lead to embarrassment.

You lead your partner in the same way that you might drive a well-liked car. You must anticipate change of direction so that you can give the cue for change just previous to the actual change. You cue your partner generally through one or more of the following methods:

A. CHEST OR BODY WEIGHT

Shifting weight before stepping with some body pressure in moving forward. This indicates backward motion for your partner.

Regular Open Position.   *Closed Position.*

Separated Position.

Conversation Position.

B. ARM AND HAND PRESSURE

1. *Leading partner in backward direction:*

Press partner's right hand with your left and release pressure of the right hand on partner's back.

2. *Leading partner in forward direction:*

Pull partner toward you with right hand and release pressure of the left.

3. *Leading partner in sideward direction:*

Press hand against partner's left side.

4. *Changing positions:*

a. *Regular open and conversation position:*

Press heel of right hand into partner's back and turn your shoulders left.

b. *Right open reverse position:*

Press heel of right hand in partner's back, push partner's right hand with your left, and turn your body so that your left side is next to your partner's left side.

c. *Left open reverse position:*

Press fingers of right hand in partner's back, push with left hand, and turn so that your right sides are together.

Right Reverse Position.   *Left Reverse Position.*

FOLLOWING

To know both the lead and the follow positions is to have a much better understanding of the problems of your partner; you will experience many different problems with many different partners. By knowing how to follow as well as lead, you will develop more skill in social dancing. A certain amount of skill is important both to your security on the dance floor and to your popularity.

To follow well, you must be relaxed but not collapsed. When you are relaxed, you are more flexible and co-operative. A good job of following is achieved by mastering the points listed below:

A. BALANCE

You must be sure that your weight is carried over the balls of the feet and that it is shifted with each step—not after the step is taken.

B. WEIGHT

Be sure to support your own weight. Be ready to move, but let the person leading take the initiative to do the moving. You do not step simultaneously with your partner but, rather, a fraction of a second after the lead is taken.

C. KNOWLEDGE

There is no substitute for knowing many steps. Practice them until you are skilled enough to do them without concentrating.

D. EXPERIENCE

The more experience you can get dancing with many different partners, the more proficient you will become. There is no substitute for experience, and the greater the variety, the better the results. Remember, even though you are more skilled than your partner, do not attempt to lead or teach him.

TECHNIQUE TIPS

1. Stand as tall as possible.
2. Move in one piece—solid, but not stiff.
3. Keep your weight over the balls of the feet.
4. Be definite in transferring weight. He who hesitates is likely to trip.
5. Relax. The first signs of tension appear in hiking the shoulders and holding your partner's hand too tightly.
6. Look at your partner or beyond —never at your feet.
7. Step with the whole leg—from the hip—not from the knee.
8. Make sure that your steps are directly forward, backward, sideward, or diagonal.

9. Place the feet accurately—don't throw the legs.
10. Be ready to recover to a standing position when you do dip figures. The time to relax is not on the dip.
11. Men always begin with the left foot; women begin on the right. Be ready to start with the correct foot.
12. Hold your partner gently but firmly.

CUES ON MANNERS

1. Consideration of your partner and others is of first importance in social dancing.
2. A gentleman escorts his partner to her seat or to her group of friends following a dance.
3. Be direct but polite in asking a girl to dance. Ask the kind of question that she can respond to with a definite answer.
4. Take the space you need but not at the expense of others.

FUNDAMENTAL SKILLS OF SOCIAL DANCING

One of the hardest skills to teach anyone is that of walking. Somehow, we take walking for granted because we have been doing it all our lives. The fact of the matter is that few people walk either correctly or efficiently. Consequently, the first point of concentration should be on walking.

DANCE WALK

Let's start from a good standing position. This means: stand tall, suck in the abdomen, lift the chest, relax the shoulders, and make sure that the body weight is over the balls of the feet. To begin walking, press the body forward as you reach forward with the leg. Let the toes reach along the floor as you step. The step must be taken with the whole leg—not from the knee. The same applies to moving backward. Reach backward from the hip and take a full stride, reaching with the toe.

DIP

Dip figures can be done either forward or backward. The backward dip is generally taken by the man. As he steps backward, he bends the knee and "sits" into the hip, holding his weight in the thigh. The other leg is stretched and the knee that is bent is turned slightly outward. For the woman, the knee is bent as she steps forward and the weight is carried in the thigh. The left leg is extended diagonally backward. The body is straight, as is the man's—there is no tilting of the body in a dip. The woman's knee falls to the inside of her partner's (see page 29).

DRAW STEP

In a draw step, the foot is brought to a closed position without the transfer of weight. In the draw, the moving foot is kept in contact with the floor.

Dance Walk.

"Dip."

ROCK STEP

A rock step is done simply by shifting the weight onto one foot and quickly shifting it back to the other foot. The feet do not change position. The rock is generally done forward or backward.

OPPOSITION HIP SHIFT

The opposition hip shift is done by taking a step (without weight) left as the hips are shifted to the right, and just the reverse; the step must be separated from the shift of weight, which goes in the direction opposite to the step.

Following, you will find the various positions used in social dancing. Learn these positions now. Practice them with your partner, changing from one to another with the proper leading cues (see pages 24-26).

ABBREVIATED SYMBOLS AND THEIR MEANING

In order to keep the description of social dance figures brief and simple, the following abbreviations have been adopted:

Rhythms	Meaning
S	Slow
Q	Quick
q	Quick (faster than Q)

Step Patterns	Meaning
L	Left foot
R	Right foot
Cl	Close
Sl	Slide
H	Hop
Hd	Hold

Direction	
FWD . . .	Forward
BKWD . .	Backward
SDWD . .	Sideward
CC	Counterclockwise
CW	Clockwise

In all steps, the weight is shifted with the step unless specified otherwise.

Counts. Counts separated by commas, as in *1, 2,* mean that the steps in succession take those counts. When numbers appear with a dash between them, *1–2,* it means that the step takes that amount of time. Often this includes holding a count. When numbers are separated by "and" (*1 and 2*), it means that the first count is divided into two parts, the first consisting of *1 and.*

FOXTROT

The foxtrot step is basic to all other steps because it uses a straight walk with fast and slow rhythms. Actually, it is best described as walking in 4/4 time. It utilizes both slow and quick steps, and the dancers are fairly free to

make their own combinations spontaneously.

There is some discrepancy between what some people consider a basic foxtrot step and what other people think about it. To some, a basic foxtrot consists of the following:

Step fwd L	S
Step fwd R	S
Step sdwd L	Q
Cl R to L	Q

The problem with this organization is that the total step takes six counts, whereas the music measure you are dancing to lasts for eight counts. In other words, the musical measure does not equal the dance measure. In addition, this step is one-sided, moving you continuously into the center of the room.

The broader interpretation of a foxtrot allows more freedom to make combinations and utilizes the full eight-count measure. In order to keep the music and the dance measure even, it is necessary to add another single step to the previously described foxtrot step. Thus, the following would constitute the basic foxtrot step. This becomes the same as two single steps and a two-step (see page 11).

The above step alternates from side to side. You will note that the latter part of the basic foxtrot (step sdwd, Cl, step fwd) is known as a *two-step.*

Following is a series of foxtrot variations that may be done in combination with the basic step or with other variations. Throughout this section the directions are given for the man. The woman does the counterpart except when specifically noted.

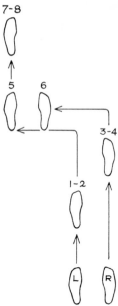

BASIC FOXTROT 4/4

Closed Position	Tempo	Count
Step fwd L	S	1-2
Step fwd R	S	3-4
Step sdwd L, Cl R to L	Q,Q	1,2
Step fwd L	S	3-4

Figure 3. Foxtrot.

CONVERSATION FIGURE

Position	Pattern	Rhythm
Open	Step fwd L	S 1-2
	Step fwd R	S 3-4
Closed	Step sdwd L, Cl R to L	Q,Q 5,6
	Step fwd L	S 7-8

Repeat, starting with
R foot.

Note: The basic step is the same. The direction and position are varied.

DIP FIGURE

Position	Pattern	Rhythm
Open	Step fwd L	S 1-2
	Step fwd R	S 3-4
Closed	Step sdwd L, Cl R to L	Q,Q 5,6
	Dip bkwd L	S 7-8

J. M. HODGES LIBRARY
WHARTON COUNTY JUNIOR COLLEGE
WHARTON, TEXAS

ROCK FIGURE [*]

Position	Pattern	Rhythm
Open	Step fwd L	S 1-2
	Step fwd R	S 3-4
	Rock fwd L, bkwd R, fwd L	Q,Q,Q 1,2,3-4

CROSS BACK REVERSE FIGURE

Position	Pattern	Rhythm
Conversation	Step fwd L	S 1-2
	Step fwd R	S 3-4
Closed	Step sdwd L	Q 1
	Cross R in back of L	Q 2
Reverse Conversation	Step bkwd L	S 3-4
	Repeat, starting R.	

CROSS-OVER FIGURE

Position	Pattern	Rhythm
Conversation	Step fwd L, step fwd R	S,S 1-2, 3-4
	Man: Rocks fwd L, bkwd R, fwd L, while	Q,Q,S 1,2,3-4
	Woman: Takes 3 steps R,L,R, crossing in front of partner to other side	
	Repeat, starting R.	

PIVOT FIGURE

Position	Pattern	Rhythm
Open	Step fwd L, step fwd R	S,S 1-2, 3-4
Closed	Turning R, step L,R,L	Q,Q,S 1,2,3-4
Open	Step fwd R, step fwd L	S,S 1-2, 3-4
	Rock bkwd R, fwd L, bkwd R	Q,Q,S 1,2, 3-4

---

[*] For rock step, see page 29.

REVERSE FIGURE

Position	Pattern	Rhythm
Left open reverse	Step fwd L, step fwd R	S,S 1-2,3-4
Closed	Step sdwd L, Cl R to L,	Q,Q 1,2
	Step fwd L	S 3-4
Right open reverse		
Closed	Step fwd R, step fwd L	S,S 1-2, 3-4
	Step sdwd R, Cl L to R,	Q,Q 1,2
	Step fwd R	S 3-4

Practice each of the variations until they become smooth. You may combine any of these figures or make up your own as you go along. Many other variations are possible.

The foxtrot is a smooth dance. You should glide across the floor very much on a smooth walking level, with the exception of dip figures. The foxtrot is characterized by long and short smooth steps.

LINDY

The Lindy dates back to 1927, when "it became our national (jazz) dance." [1] It is generally thought that the Lindy descended through jazz from the American Negro. The Lindy varies in style in different parts of the country. However, it is still identifiable in one of three forms—either the single, double, or triple Lindy. It doesn't really matter which you do, since all three are done to the same rhythm and measure. This means that two people can do the Lindy together, one doing a double or single and the other a triple. The single Lindy is not generally done but forms the basis for learning the others. It is also the foundation of the Charleston. The man's part is described. The woman's part is opposite except when specifically noted.

SINGLE LINDY 4/4

Position	Pattern	Rhythm
Regular open	Step fwd L	S 1-2
	Step bkwd R	S 3-4
	Rock bkwd L, fwd R	Q,Q 5,6

Figure 4. Single Lindy.

[1] Marshall Stern, "On Rock and Roll." New York: Glamour Magazine, July 1958, p. 18.

DOUBLE LINDY

Position	Pattern	Rhythm
Regular open	Tap L, step fwd L	Q,Q 1,2
	Tap R, step bkwd R	Q,Q 3,4
	Rock bkwd L, fwd R	Q,Q 5,6

TRIPLE LINDY

Position	Pattern	Rhythm
Regular open	Step L fwd, Cl R to L, step L fwd	q,q,q 1&2
	Step R bkwd, Cl L to R, step R bkwd	q,q,q 3&4
	Rock bkwd L	Q 5
	Rock fwd R	Q 6

SIMPLE BREAK

A *break* is a change of step, and in this case a change of position from the basic step so that free variation is possible. From closed position you move diagonally backward—away from your partner—with the following:

Triple Lindy L
Triple Lindy R
Rock bkwd L, fwd R

Another simple break is for the man to take two Lindy steps in place and swing the girl with his left hand to turn her clockwise to a separated position. Once in a separated position, you are free to improvise. To get together again, take six steps, each starting with the toe out and turning it in as the weight is taken on that foot.

BOOGIE FIGURE

Position	Pattern	Rhythm
Separated	Small leap fwd L, Cl R to L, clapping hands after the Cl.	q,q & 1 2
	Small leap bkwd L, Cl R to L, clapping hands after the Cl.	q,q & 3 4
	Circle L knee, keeping toe in place.	S 1-2
	Circle R knee, keeping toe in place.	S 3-4

WRAP-AROUND FIGURE

Position	Pattern	Rhythm
Closed with hands joined across	Double Lindy, starting L, loop woman's L hand overhead ending with her L arm across and in front of her waist and her R arm in man's left. Man's R arm is around her waist.	q,q, q,q 1&2& 3,4
	Rock bkwd R and fwd L	Q,Q 5,6
	Double Lindy L, turning woman under L arm back to starting position.	

PUSH-AWAY FIGURE (TRIPLE LINDY)

Position	Pattern	Rhythm
Closed with hands touching	Two-step L with arms extending sdwd	q,q,q 1&2
	Two-step R with arms extending sdwd	q,q,q 3&4
	Rock bkwd L and fwd R, bringing arms in and separating couple.	Q,Q 5,6

SPIN FIGURE (TRIPLE LINDY)

Position	Pattern	Rhythm
Closed	Two-step L sdwd	q,q,q 1&2
	Two-step R sdwd	q,q,q 3&4
	Man: Turns CC in two steps, L R	Q,Q 5,6
	Woman: Turns CW in two steps, R L	

Note: On the spin in this figure, the man cues the woman for the turn by pressing the heel of his right hand in her back and dropping the extended arm.

CHA CHA CHA

The Cha Cha Cha is often referred to as the triple or simplified Mambo. This derives from the fact that the count of four and the holdover to count one of the next measure in Mambo turns into the action of three quick steps in Cha Cha Cha. It is much easier to do something definite with the feet than to hold rhythm. The tempo of the Cha Cha Cha is also slower than Mambo. The three quick shuffle steps that give Cha Cha Cha its character fall on counts four and one. Once again you have the subtlety of Cuban rhythm. You will see few people beginning to step on count two— habit dictates beginning on count one. The man's part is described. The woman's part is opposite except when spefically noted.

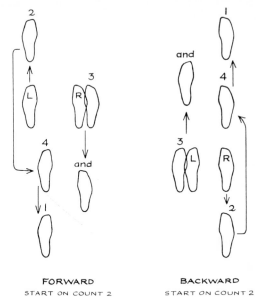

FORWARD
START ON COUNT 2

BACKWARD
START ON COUNT 2

Figure 5.   Cha Cha Cha.

BASIC CHA CHA CHA 4/4

Position	Pattern	Rhythm
Closed or separated	Step fwd L, step bkwd R	S,S 2,3
	Three small, quick steps bkwd, L,R,L	q,q,q 4&1
	Step bkwd R, step fwd L	S,S 2,3
	Three small, quick steps fwd R,L,R	q,q,q 4&1

SIDEWARD FIGURE

Position	Pattern	Rhythm
Closed	Step fwd L, step bkwd R	S,S 2,3
	Step sdwd L, Cl R to L, sdwd L	q,q,q 4&1
	Step bkwd R, step fwd L	S,S 2,3
	Step sdwd R, Cl L to R, step sdwd R	q,q,q 4&1

SIDE BREAK FIGURE

Position	Pattern	Rhythm
Closed	Step sdwd L, step R in place	S,S 1,2
	Cl L to R, step in place R, L	q,q,q 3&4
	Repeat, starting sdwd R.	

Note: On the repeat, the woman may turn in place clockwise on two slow steps while the man does the regular side break.

CHARGE STEP FIGURE

Position	Pattern	Rhythm
Separated	Lunge L foot across R, kicking up R heel.	S 1
	Step in place R	S 2
	Step sdwd L, Cl R to L, step sdwd L	q,q,q 3&4
	Repeat, starting R.	

Note: Let the shoulders and whole body turn on the lunge and bend the knee. Try putting a CC turn for the woman on the three short steps.

CHASE FIGURE

Position	Pattern	Rhythm
Separated	Man: Step fwd L, pivoting ½ turn CW	S 1
	Step in place R	S 2
	Three short steps fwd L,R,L	q,q,q 3&4
	Woman: Step bkwd R, step fwd L	S,S 1,2
	Three short steps fwd	q,q,q 3&4
	R,L,R (Man's back is to woman's face)	
	Man: Step fwd L, pivoting ½ turn CC, step in place R	S 1 S 2
	Three short steps fwd L,R,L	q,q,q 3&4

Note: Man and woman are now doing the same thing single file. A tap on the shoulder before you pivot when you are in back of your partner adds to the flirtation character of the chase. To get back to starting position, the man stops the pivot normally done on the left foot forward; his partner then turns automatically, and you are facing each other again.

BOX FIGURE

Position	Pattern	Rhythm
Closed	Step sdwd L, Cl R to L	S,S 1,2
	Step sdwd L, Cl R to L,	
	step fwd L	q,q,q 3&4
	Step sdwd R, Cl L to R	S,S 1,2
	Step sdwd R, Cl L to R,	
	step bkwd R	q,q,q 3&4

Note: This may be done in separated position, with the woman dropping backward and toward her partner, instead of in the parallel form shown.

The Cha Cha Cha is an accented shuffle step. The body is straight, arms bent at elbows when separated. The arms may be used freely but generally are limited to a shoulder-rolling kind of motion.

MAMBO

The basic Mambo step is believed to be derived from the Cuban Rhumba, even though the two appear to be very dissimilar. The Mambo has much of the same quality as the Rhumba. The movement is initiated in the hips, as in the Rhumba, but it is not quite so subtle as Rhumba. Mambo uses the same rhythmic measure but with the first count of every four held. This presents problems, because habit dictates movement on count one. When you move on one, you hold count four. You will probably see few couples starting Mambo on count two, but that is the way it should be done. Holding count one and moving on the usually unaccented beat of count two help to produce the quality of hip movement of Mambo, which should be subtle and syncopated. You will note below that the rhythmic pattern is even: each step gets the same amount of time. The man's part is described. The woman's part is opposite except when specifically noted.

BASIC MAMBO

Position	Pattern	Rhythm
Closed	Step fwd L	Q 2
	Step bkwd R	Q 3
	Cl L to R	S 4-1
	Step bkwd R	Q 2
	Step fwd L	Q 3
	Cl R to L	S 4-1

FORWARD   BACKWARD

Figure 6.   Mambo.

Note: The rhythm of quick, quick, slow relates to counts two, three, and four with the holdover of the first count as part of the slow. Bend the knee as you take the first quick step.

SIDE BREAK

Position	Pattern	Rhythm
Closed	Step L sdwd	Q 2
	Step R in place	Q 3
	Cl L to R	S 4-1
	Repeat, starting R sdwd.	S 4-1

CROSSOVER FIGURE

Position	Pattern	Rhythm
Closed	One sdwd break L	Q,Q,S 2,3,4-1
	Man: Sdwd break R	Q,Q,S 2,3,4-1
	Woman: Step R,L,R, turning under man's left arm and ending on his left side.	
Open	Man: Step fwd L, bkwd R, in place L	Q,Q,S 2,3,4-1
	Woman: Step fwd R, bkwd L, in place R	
	Man: Step sdwd L, Cl R to L, step sdwd L	Q,Q,S 2,3,4-1
	Woman: Step R,L,R, turning and crossing to partner's R side. Man takes her L hand in his R as she crosses.	

SIMPLE BREAK

Position	Pattern	Rhythm
Closed	One basic step fwd on L Man: Step bkwd R, Cl L to R, step R in place, releasing partner's left hand Woman: Step bkwd L, Cl R to L, step L in place	Q,Q,S 2,3,4-1 Q,Q,S 2,3,4-1

CROSS-TURN FIGURE

Position	Pattern	Rhythm
Separated	Step L in place, cross R over L in front, step in place L	Q,Q,S 2,3,4-1
	Repeat cross step, starting R	Q,Q,S 2,3,4-1
	Repeat cross step, starting L	Q,Q,S 2,3,4-1
	Man: Turns CW in place L,R,L Woman: Turns CC in place L,R,L	Q,Q,S 2,3,4-1

COMBO FIGURE

Position	Pattern	Rhythm
Conversation	Man: Sdwd break L Woman: Step R,L,R turning CC to face partner.	Q,Q,S 2,3,4-1
Separated	Man: Step bkwd R, fwd L, Cl R to L Woman: Step fwd L, bkwd R, Cl L to R	Q,Q,S 2,3,4-1
	Man: Sdwd break L, taking girl's L hand with his R Woman: Turns CW R,L,R under her own arm	Q,Q,S 2,3,4-1
	Man: Step bkwd R, fwd L, Cl R to L Woman: Step fwd L, bkwd R, Cl L to R	Q,Q,S 2,3,4-1

RHUMBA

The Rhumba is the subtlest of Cuban dances. This is a dance in which all the action is initiated in the hips. The feet stay on the floor, the knees are flexible, the body is lifted, and the action is small. Consequently, you do not travel very far. The co-ordination of hip action is what makes a Rhumba, and it also makes it difficult to learn. The action in the hips is from side to side, even though the step goes sideward and forward or sideward and backward. The step precedes the shift of weight. You take the step on the beat without the weight and you shift your weight after the beat as you begin the next step. This produces the opposition hip shift—the hips are shifting in the direction opposite to the step. Closed position for Rhumba varies from the usual in that the man's right hand is at the woman's left side at the waist and his left hand

is up and forward with the elbow bent. The woman's forearm is against the man's and his fingers fold over the woman's finger tips (see page 24). The man's part is described for the following steps. The woman's part is opposite except when specifically noted. Remember to shift the weight after you have taken the step.

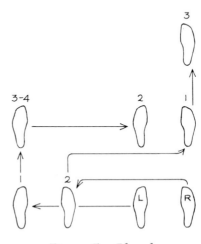

Figure 7. Rhumba.

BASIC RHUMBA 4/4

Position	Pattern	Rhythm
Closed	Step sdwd L	Q 1
	Cl R to L	Q 2
	Step fwd L and hold	S 3-4
	Step sdwd R	Q 1
	Cl L to R	Q 2
	Step fwd R and hold	S 3-4

BOX FIGURE

Position	Pattern	Rhythm
Closed	Step sdwd L, Cl R to L, step fwd L and hold	Q,Q,S 1,2,3-4
	Step sdwd R, Cl L to R, step bkwd R and hold	Q,Q,S 1,2,3-4

SIDE BREAK

Position	Pattern	Rhythm
Closed	Point L foot sdwd	Q 1
	Cl L to R (no weight)	Q 2
	Step L in place and hold	S 3-4
	Repeat, starting R	

TURNING FIGURE

Position	Pattern	Rhythm
Closed	Step L sdwd, Cl R to L	Q,Q 1,2
	Pivot ¼ turn CC by turning L foot outward and leaving R behind L	S 3-4
	Step R sdwd, Cl L to R	Q,Q 1,2
	Pivot ¼ turn CC by turning R foot inward as you step bkwd on it.	S 3-4
	Repeat all to complete one full turn.	

BREAK FIGURES

Position	Pattern	Rhythm
Closed	Forward: Step L fwd, R in place, and L in place. Woman swings out bkwd to a separated position.	Q,Q,S 1,2,3-4
	Backward: Step bkwd L, step in place R, in place L.	Q,Q,S 1,2,3-4

Note: The man uses his left hand to press woman away and also the heel of his right hand at her waist to indicate a break.

CIRCLE RUN FIGURE

Position	Pattern	Rhythm
Conversation with both hands at shoulder height	Man: steps bkwd as pivot point L,R,L, hold; R,L,R, hold.	Q,Q,S 1,2,3-4
	Woman: travels around man with R,L,R, hold; L,R,L, hold. Woman's left hand is in man's right.	Q,Q,S 1,2,3-4

RIGHT AND LEFT OPEN REVERSE FIGURE

Position	Pattern	Rhythm
Closed	Two basic steps fwd.	Q,Q,S 1,2,3-4
		Q,Q,S 1,2,3-4
	Forward break.	Q,Q,S 1,2,3-4
Left Open Reverse	Three steps pivoting CW.	Q,Q,S 1,2,3-4
	Repeat twice.	
Right Open Reverse	Pivot CC with basic step fwd for man and bkwd for woman four times.	Q,Q,S 1,2,3-4

Note: Maintain the hip shift on circle runs. Keep steps small. To change from left to right, reverse change on the hold by pivoting and step into the new position on the beginning of the next step.

Rhumba is an elegant dance with subtle expressions. The upper body is held high and does not move. The step is initiated by subtle hip action. The feet are kept close to the floor, the weight being shifted on the whole foot. Steps should be small; you do not travel very far with Rhumba steps.

SAMBA

The Samba comes from Brazil. It differs from the other Latin-American dances in that it is lively and vigorous and the feet are constantly leaving the floor. It is literally a bouncing step. The basic step pattern is similar to the waltz balance, but the feeling and quality of movement are quite different. The movement of Samba uses the whole body. The upper body tilts forward as the feet go backward. The spirit of Samba is light and gay. The steps are small, the bouncing is light, and the knees are kept flexible. Dance position for Samba is the same as that for Rhumba. The man's part is described here. The woman's part is opposite except when specifically noted.

BASIC SAMBA 2/4

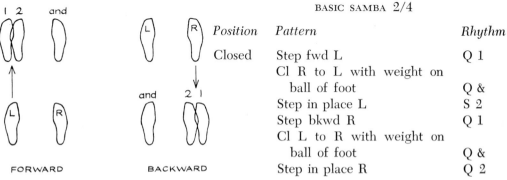

Figure 8. Samba.

Position	Pattern	Rhythm
Closed	Step fwd L	Q 1
	Cl R to L with weight on ball of foot	Q &
	Step in place L	S 2
	Step bkwd R	Q 1
	Cl L to R with weight on ball of foot	Q &
	Step in place R	Q 2

TURN FIGURE

Position	*Pattern*	*Rhythm*
Closed	The basic step is used for turning. Man's L steps slightly outward on the fwd step and R foot slightly inward on bkwd step. Turn is achieved by this gradual process. The reverse is true for CW turn. Man should lean in direction of turn, dropping L shoulder for L turn, R shoulder for R turn.	Q,Q,S 1 & 2

CROSS-STEP FIGURE

Position	*Pattern*	*Rhythm*
Closed	Step L across R	Q 1
	Step R sdwd (sm. step)	Q &
	Cl L to R	S 2
	Step R across L	Q 1
	Step L sdwd (sm. step)	Q &
	Cl R to L	S 2

Note: Let the body turn in the direction of the cross step and face partner squarely on the side-close step.

SWING-AWAY FIGURE

Position	*Pattern*	*Rhythm*
Separated with hands touching	Step L in place	Q 1
	Cross R in back of L turning the body away from partner (woman CC, man CW) with man's L hand joined with woman's R.	Q &
	Step in place L, facing partner.	S 2
	Repeat, starting R and swinging in opposite direction.	

DRAG FIGURE

Position	Pattern	Rhythm
Conversation	Man: Step fwd L, step in place R, drag L to R Woman: Step fwd R, in place L, drag R to L Repeat, starting with oppo-site foot.	Q,Q,S 1&2

Note: This can be done in place or it can be used as a forward traveling step by taking a large first step and taking the second step slightly forward.

COMBINATION FIGURE

Position	Pattern	Rhythm
Closed Separated	8 basic steps, starting L	1-16
	8 cross-step figures, with man and woman both crossing in front (man places R fore-arm against woman's L forearm).	1-16
	Drag figure 8 times, with the woman swinging under man's arm in a CW turn on the 8th step to arrive in closed position.	1-16

The body swing in Samba takes place from the waist down. The upper body tilts forward and backward while the legs swing under the body to step forward and backward.

WALTZ

The waltz, a regal and graceful dance, differs from other steps not only in quality but in rhythm. The waltz is done in three beats. Each beat is equal to the others (except in Viennese waltzing). The first beat of each three is accented. When you waltz beautifully, you have the sensation of floating on air and you cover distance with the greatest of ease. The man's part is described here. The woman's part is opposite except when specifically noted.

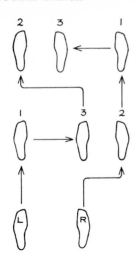

Figure 9.   Waltz.

BASIC WALTZ 3/4

Position	Pattern	Rhythm
Closed	Step fwd L	S 1
	Step sdwd R	S 2
	Cl L to R	S 3
	Step fwd R	S 1
	Step sdwd L	S 2
	Cl R to L	S 3

BOX WALTZ FIGURE

Position	Pattern	Rhythm
Closed	Step fwd L, sdwd R,	
	Cl L to R	S,S,S 1,2,3
	Step bkwd R, sdwd L,	
	Cl R to L	S,S,S 1,2,3

WALTZ TURN FIGURE

Position	Pattern	Rhythm
Closed	Step fwd L, pivoting ¼ turn	
	CC	S 1
	Step sdwd R	S 2
	Cl L to R	S 3
	Step bkwd R, turning leg in-	
	ward and pivoting ¼ turn	
	CC	S 1
	Step sdwd L	S 2
	Cl R to L	S 3
	Repeat from beginning to	
	complete one full turn.	

Note: The pivot may also be ½ turn.

PURSUIT WALTZ FIGURE

Position	Pattern	Rhythm
Closed	One basic waltz fwd L	S,S,S 1,2,3
Left Open Reverse	Step fwd R, diagonally fwd L, Cl R to L	S,S,S 1,2,3
Right Open Reverse	Step fwd L, diagonally fwd R, Cl L to R	S,S,S 1,2,3
	Repeat from left open reverse as long as desired.	

BALANCE FIGURE

Position	Pattern	Rhythm
Closed	Step fwd L, Cl R to L, step in place L	S,S,S 1,2,3
	Step bkwd R, Cl L to R, step in place R	S,S,S 1,2,3

WALTZ CORTÉ FIGURE

Position	Pattern	Rhythm
Closed	Two basic waltz steps fwd, starting L	S,S,S 1,2,3 S,S,S 1,2,3
	Dip bkwd	S 1-3
	One waltz step fwd R	S,S,S 1,2,3

TANGO

Of all the Latin-American dances, the Tango stands out with a distinction and fascination all its own. It derives from Argentina, although it has undergone many changes since its beginnings, and consequently has lost some of its original characteristics.

Tango has a slithering quality. It is smooth, with very distinct accents. The steps are elongated and the music strongly creates the mood of the dance. The upper body should be carried high and direction changes well marked. The steps should be smooth and deliberate but subtle. The body is stretched and has the proud characteristics reminiscent of the bull-fighter. The man's part is described here. The woman's part is opposite except when specifically noted.

J. M. HODGES LIBRARY
WHARTON COUNTY JUNIOR COLLEGE
WHARTON, TEXAS

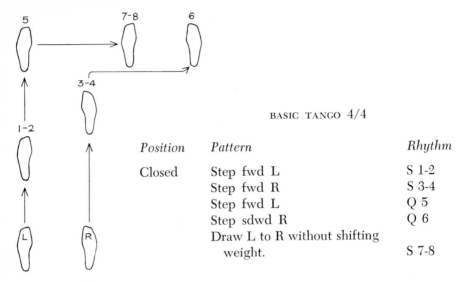

BASIC TANGO 4/4

Position	Pattern	Rhythm
Closed	Step fwd L	S 1-2
	Step fwd R	S 3-4
	Step fwd L	Q 5
	Step sdwd R	Q 6
	Draw L to R without shifting weight.	S 7-8

Figure 10.   Tango.

Note: The basic step is more interestingly done on the diagonal, changing from right open reverse to left open reverse.

SIDE FIGURE

Position	Pattern	Rhythm
Open	Step fwd L, step fwd R	S,S 1-2, 3-4
Closed	Step fwd L, step sdwd R	Q,Q 5,6
	Draw L to R	S 7-8

CROSS-SIDE FIGURE

Position	Pattern	Rhythm
Open	Step fwd L, step fwd R	S,S 1-2, 3-4
Regular Open Reverse	Man: Cross L in front of R, step sdwd R, close L to R	Q,Q,S 5,6, 7-8
	Woman: Cross R in front (or back) of L, step sdwd L, draw R to L	

DIP FIGURE

Position	Pattern	Rhythm
Closed	Dip bkwd L, step fwd R	S,S 1-2, 3-4
	Step fwd L, sdwd R	Q,Q 5,6
	Draw L to R	S 7-8

CROSS FIGURE, FRONT AND BACK

Position	Pattern	Rhythm
Open	Step fwd L, step fwd R	S,S 1-2, 3-4
	Cross L in back of R	Q 5
	Step sdwd R	Q 6
	Cross L in front of R	Q 7
	Step sdwd R	Q 8
	Repeat twice.	
	Take one basic tango step.	

LONGSIDE FIGURE

Position	Pattern	Rhythm
Open	Step fwd L, step fwd R	S,S 1-2, 3-4
	Step fwd L, step fwd R	Q,Q 5,6
	Step fwd L	S 7-8
	Step in place R	S 1-2
	Cross L in back of R.	S 3-4
Closed	Step sdwd R	Q 5
	Cross L in front of R	Q 6
	Bring R toe in wide circle CC	
	around L	S 7-8
	Step R fwd	S 1-2
	Step L, turning ¼ L	Q 3
	Step sdwd R	Q 4
	Draw L to R for four counts.	S 5-8

MERENGUE

The Merengue derives from a folk dance of the Dominican Republic and was adapted to social dancing. The Merengue has been a popular dance in its native country for some time, but its popularity in the United States is recent. The Merengue is very much like the one-step going sideward. However, the quality and character of the movement and music are distinctly Carib-

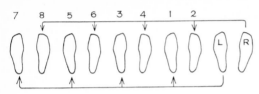

Figure 11.   Merengue.

tion hip shift is present in the Merengue as it is in the true Cuban Rhumba. It is a dance initiated in the hips with the knees kept flexible. The steps are very small and taken on the whole foot. The man's part is described here. The woman's part is opposite except when specifically noted.

bean. It is a dance that is confined to a small amount of space. The opposi-

BASIC MERENGUE 2/4 OR 4/4

Position	Pattern	Rhythm
Closed	Step sdwd L as you shift hips R sdwd.	S 1
	Cl R to L as you shift hips L sdwd.	S 2
	Repeat three times from beginning.	3-8

TURN FIGURE

Position	Pattern	Rhythm
Closed	Step fwd L, turning leg ⅛ turn outward.	S 1
	Bring R to L but slightly behind.	S 2
	Step sdwd L, Cl R to L	S,S 3,4
	Repeat from beginning.	

ROCK FIGURE

Position	Pattern	Rhythm
Closed	Step sdwd L, Cl R to L, stepping in front of L.	S,S 1,2
	Step sdwd L, bring R to L, not closing.	S,S 3,4
	Cross L in back of R, step R in place.	S,S 5,6
	Step L sdwd, Cl R to L.	S,S 7,8

BOX FIGURE

Position	Pattern	Rhythm
Closed	Step fwd L	S 1
	Step sdwd R	S 2
	Cl L to R	S 3
	Step bkwd R	S 4

PIVOT TURN FIGURE

Position	Pattern	Rhythm
Closed	Step fwd L	S 1
	Step in place R, turning	
	¼ CW	S 2
	Step fwd L	S 3
	Step in place R, turning	
	¼ CW	S 4

Repeat to complete a full
turn.

Note: The left foot actually describes the circle with the forward steps. The right foot stays in one place and acts as a pivot point.

CROSS-BACK FIGURE

Position	Pattern	Rhythm
Separated	Cross L behind R	S 1
	Step sdwd R (sm. step)	S 2
	Cl L to R	S 3
	Step in place R	S 4

CALYPSO

Calypso is a unique type of dance that stems from the folk dance of the British West Indies. The Calypso folk dance is a true and very basic expression of the Negro population of that area. The social form of Calypso is an adaptation in which steps are patterned. This patterning in itself tends to destroy the spontaneous quality found in the folk form. The opposition hip shift (see page 29) is present again in Calypso, but here it is a freer swing of the hips with a repercussion in the upper body. The steps themselves are simple. The man's part is described. The woman's part is opposite except when specifically noted.

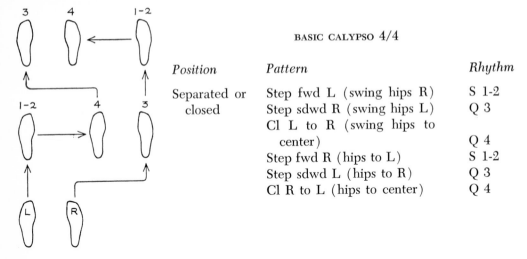

BASIC CALYPSO 4/4

Position	Pattern	Rhythm
Separated or closed	Step fwd L (swing hips R)	S 1-2
	Step sdwd R (swing hips L)	Q 3
	Cl L to R (swing hips to center)	Q 4
	Step fwd R (hips to L)	S 1-2
	Step sdwd L (hips to R)	Q 3
	Cl R to L (hips to center)	Q 4

Figure 12. Calypso.

Note: Steps are small and on the whole foot. The hip swing continues in opposition to the step but is always a sideward swing. The hip movement should be subtle.

PROMENADE FIGURE

Position	Pattern	Rhythm
Conversation	Step fwd L (no weight, hips R)	S 1-2
	Step fwd R, taking weight L (hips to the L)	S 3-4
	Repeat six times.	

SIDEWARD FIGURE

Position	Pattern	Rhythm
Separated	Step L sdwd	S 1-2
	Step R sdwd, Cl L to R	Q,Q 3,4
	Step R sdwd	S 1-2
	Step L sdwd, Cl R to L	Q,Q 3,4

Note: On the slow sideward step, the body should swing and pivot slightly in a backward direction.

BOX FIGURE

Position	Pattern	Rhythm
Closed	One basic figure fwd	S,Q,Q 1-2, 3,4
	One basic figure bkwd	S,Q,Q 1-2, 3,4

LADY'S BREAK AND TURN FIGURE

Position	Pattern	Rhythm
Closed	One basic figure fwd L	S,Q,Q 1-2, 3,4
	One basic step fwd R	S,Q,Q 1-2, 3,4
	Man: One complete box figure, releasing partner's waist and leading with left hand.	
	Woman: Turn under man's L hand with a step bkwd R.	S 1-2
	Step fwd L, Cl R to L	Q,Q 3,4
	Step fwd L, sdwd R, Cl L to R	S,Q,Q 1-2, 3,4

CONVERSATION FIGURE

Position	Pattern	Rhythm
Separated	Four sdwd figures, starting L	1-16
	Eight promenade steps, clapping hands on off beat.	1-16
	Free conversation in movement. Use actions or gestures toward partner.	1-16
	Repeat sdwd figures.	1-16

SELECTED RECORDINGS FOR SOCIAL DANCING

Calypso

Victor LPM-1248,   Decca 8159
   1150   Paragon 604
Columbia CL-928

Cha Cha Cha

Victor 23-6232,   * EDA-SD-7
   23-6206, 23-6563   Victor LPM-1389
Victor LPM-1392

---

* EDA-SD series, see Educational Dance Recordings, under "Record Dealers" in Appendix.

Foxtrot

Victor LPM-1070   Capitol T-258
EDA-SD-1   (LP-Murray)

Rhumba

Decca A-459   EDA-SD-4
Columbia 37556   Capitol T-259
Victor LPM-1069   (LP-Murray)
                                      Capitol CD-259
                                        (AC-78)

Lindy

Columbia 38062   EDA-SD-5
Victor LPM-1071

Samba

Columbia 38244   EDA-SD-8
Victor LPM-1073   Capitol CD-260
                                        (A1-78)

Mambo

Victor LPM-1067   Victor LPM-1389
EDA-SD-2   Capitol CD-261
Victor LPM-1075   (AC-78)

Tango

Decca A-455, 63902   EDA-SD-6
Victor LPM-1068   Capitol T-263
                                        (LP-Murray)

Waltz

Capitol 15688, 262   EDA-SD-3
  (Album)   Capitol CD-262
Victor LPM-1066   (A1-78)

Merengue

Victor 23-6415,   EDA-SD-9
  23-6515, 23-6546

SELECTED SOURCES FOR SOCIAL DANCING

American Rumba Committee, *The American Rhumba.* New York: Tudor Publishing Co., Inc., 1943.

Ballwebber, Edith, *Group Instruction in Social Dancing.* Ronald Press, 1938. Out of print.

Barrows, Frank, *Theory and Technique of Latin-American Dancing.* London: Muller, 1948.

Barry, Guy, *How to Dance the Rhumba.* New York: Kamin Dance Bookshop, 1953.

Carner, Mosco, *The Waltz.* New York: Chanticleer Press, 1948.

Castle, Vernon and Irene Foote, *Modern Dancing.* New York: Harper and Bros., 1914.

Franks, Arthur Henry, *The Ballroom Dancer's Handbook.* London: Pitman, 1947.

Hall, Willard (compiler), *Bibliography of Social Dancing.* Hastings-on-Hudson, New York, 1940.

Harris, Jane A., Anne Pittman, and Marlys S. Waller, *Dance A While*, 2nd ed. Minneapolis: Burgess Pub. Co., 1950.

Hess, Charlotte, *The Joy of Dancing: A Primer of Technique of Inner Body Weight Shifts in Social Dancing.* New York: Dance Books, 1953.

Holland, James, *Modern Ballroom Dancing.* London: Bear, Hudson Ltd., 1945.

Hostetler, Laurence A., *Walk Your Way to Better Dancing.* New York: Ronald Press, 1942.

Moore, Alexander, *Ballroom Dancing*, 6th ed. New York: Pitman Publishing Co., 1951.

Petrides, Dimitr, *The Latin-American Dances*. London: D. Petrides, 1949.

Silvester, Victor, *Modern Ballroom Dancing*, rev. ed., New York: Wahman Bros., 1953.

Waglow, I. F., *Social Dance for Students and Teachers*. Dubuque, Iowa: W. C. Brown Co., 1953.

White, Betty, *Dancing Made Easy*. New York: McKay Co., Inc., 1953.

—————, *How to Mambo*. New York: McKay Co., Inc., 1955.

—————, *Teen-age Dance Book*. New York: McKay Co., Inc., 1952.

Wright, A. P., and Wester Wright, *How to Dance*, rev. ed. New York: The New Home Library, 1952.

J. M. HODGES LIBRARY
WHARTON COUNTY JUNIOR COLLEGE
WHARTON, TEXAS

CHAPTER V

Folk Dance

Folk dances are dances that are the expressions of various ethnological groups of people. They are rhythmic expressions in movement and song. The range and variation of folk dancing are extensive, reflecting the lives of people in various parts of the world. Folk dancing is a natural form of expression, and much of the folk dancing that we know originated spontaneously. The characteristics of the various cultural groups exist because of the situations in which they live—because of their cultural mores and patterns, the climate, geographical location, work patterns, racial origins, and religious and social traditions. All of these elements influence the way men think, believe, and live, and consequently they affect their expressions of play.

Many attempts have been made to organize folk dancing into national types. Although these efforts had a purpose at one time, such classification is unsatisfactory today, owing to the displacement and moving about of large groups of people as a result of war, threats, and persecution. One can no longer think in terms of "pure" forms of folk dance that can be attributed to specific countries, because the same dances are being exchanged, shared, adapted, and adopted by groups in various countries, with the identity of the original becoming clouded, lost, or adapted. It is difficult at the present time to gather historical information that is at all valid concerning the old dances, let alone keep up with the trends that folk dance is taking at the present time. The world is becoming smaller as travel becomes more convenient and more popular, and as a jet-propelled era of excellent communications contributes to the fusion of cultures and the sharing of expression. Such rapid changes also contribute to the fading of the knowledge of the history or background of the various older folk dances. Although a wealth of folk dances are available, little information on the history or background of these dances exists.

While more information is to be desired, and would increase our knowledge about dance, this lack of information does not prohibit the enjoyment of dancing. It is often said that folk dance contributes to the understanding of other cultures and of other ways of living. If folk dance is an expression of the assimilated values of a culture, then the resultant dance and music carry the feelings and characteristics of these people. When we dance these dances in the spirit and style that the various cultural groups intended them to be danced, we are bound to feel something that helps us share the feelings of those people. In this way we can say that we gain an understanding of people through participating in their folk dances. If we want further specific knowledge and understanding of these people, we must seek them through the study of anthropology and history.

Folk dance is a language of movement, rhythm, and sound. When this language becomes a form of expression, it communicates feelings, ideas, and values to others. Joan Lawson, in her discussion of European folk dance, organizes people and their dances into groups on the basis of the languages spoken. She maintains that there is no such thing as a national folk dance, but that . . . "whenever the intimate relationship of movement, music and language has been maintained, the dance represents a national style."[1]

Folk dancing generally takes two forms: one that is the rural or peasant form, and one that is the more urban, ballroom form. Both types are included in the folk dances that follow. Whenever information is available for specific dances, it is included. Dances are often named for a town or in honor of a person of high status. Often, the dances do not have a specific story or message, but are danced for enjoyment on happy occasions or celebrations. This is not too different from the American folk dance. American square and round dances are danced primarily for the fun of dancing. Probably the main objective of people who do folk dancing is recreational. We feel good when we move in rhythm with others, and we enjoy the act of participating and the skill of co-ordinating smoothly with others. The dancers are free to develop their own individual style; there is plenty of room for spontaneity and subtle communication; and, most of all, dancing is just plain fun. The following collection of folk dances represents many different countries and types. They are the more popular dances that are done today. This collection is by no means inclusive of all types, but

---

[1] Joan Lawson, *European Folk Dance*. London: Pitman Press, 1953, p. 52.

it will serve to acquaint you with folk dancing.

The following diagrams are presented for ready reference as you learn the following dances. These are group formations that are referred to at the beginning of each folk dance other than the Square dance.

SQUARE DANCING (AMERICAN)

"When it comes to finding the origins of the Western Square Dance, for instance, one simply has to speculate. The dances and the calls, except in rare cases, were never written down, but were transmitted from caller to caller by the oral route. And all the footnotes and references and authorities are lost in the process."[2] The author of this statement, the late Lloyd Shaw, is rightfully thought of as the "pappy" of Western Square and Round dance. If there is any one person whose work can be called a primary source of sound information, it is Lloyd Shaw. He not only revived the dormant art of square dancing in the United States, but he contributed a sound and solid foundation for perpetuating this folk form through his research, writing, and teaching. Not to be discounted is his most outstanding characteristic—his genuine interest in people. The beautiful demonstrations by his Cheyenne Mountain dancers not only gave this country a picture of how Square and round dance should be done,

but also spread the spirit of real Americanism—its grass roots—its wholesome citizenship. Lloyd Shaw truly belongs in the hall of great Americans.

As to the probable origin of Western Square dance, he states, "I believe the two main sources to have been the New England Quadrille and the Kentucky Running Set. In addition, perhaps the Mexicans contributed something in the way of steps."[3] . . . "and lastly, I feel sure that some of the figures of the Western dance were borrowed directly from old European folk dances."[4]

The Western Square dance is the folk dance of America. It is found in two basic forms: the patter call and the singing call. The patter-call type of square dance is one in which the person directing the dance (caller) calls the figures of a dance and pads the call with themes —humorous and/or nonsensical—to fill the dead spaces. Callers generally develop a personal style of their own— some understandable and others not. An effective caller clearly gets his command for a figure across and distinguishes the instructional part of the call from the patter and fill. He moves a group easily, in rhythm, and uses enough inflection in his voice to avoid monotony. He also calls in tune with the music.

A *singing call* is a sequence of figures called to a specific piece of music. The call generally takes the melody of the music; thus, the caller must be able to carry a tune. Singing calls seem to be

---

[2] Lloyd Shaw, *Cowboy Dances.* Caldwell, Idaho: Caxton Printers, 1939, p. 25.
[3] *Ibid.*, p. 26.
[4] *Ibid.*, p. 26.

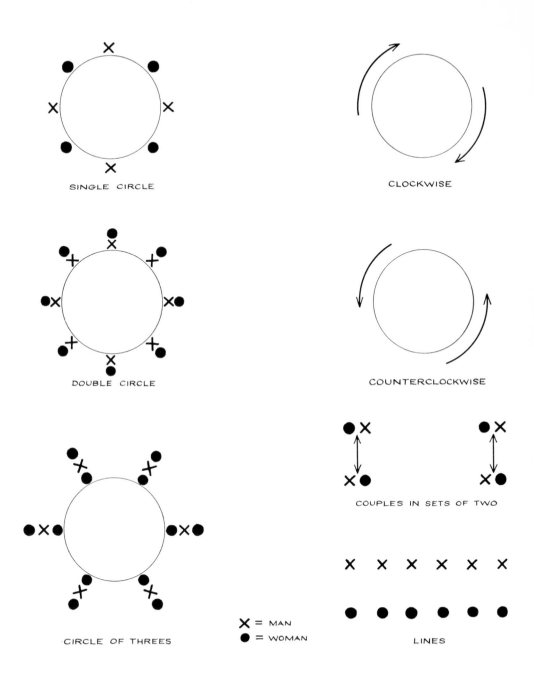

Fig. 13. *Group Formations.*

the easiest for beginners to grasp. Having to keep pace with the music gives a definite feeling of the rhythm of the dance, and it doesn't take any unusual skill to sing calls to a tune. Beginners can do this individually or in groups.

If you were to travel to different sections of the country, you would find the fundamental form of square dancing fairly consistent. However, it takes on a different look in different sections owing to local characteristics, technique, tempo, and flourishes. The patter will usually be strongly related to the life and interests of the section of the country where it is danced, but the basic figures are fairly consistent in most sections of the country.

The square dance is named for its organization in the form of a square. Four couples make up a square. They are organized as illustrated below and numbered counterclockwise around the square. Gents are X and ladies O.

This formation is the starting position and generally the finishing position. You will note that the gent is on the left of the lady. The calls are given in reference to the gents, since they are supposed to take the lead. The lady interprets her part from the call to the gent. Her part is generally opposite, but in some figures she is not included in part. In other words, both the gents and the ladies must pay close attention to the calls. The success of square dancing is dependent on each person in the square. One person can confuse the other seven. This means that you should know the figures used in a dance before dancing them. There are not very many different figures to learn. It is a simple matter to know the basic figures well enough to be able to do them spontaneously. These basic figures are explained below. If you know your left hand from your right by feel without having to look at it, you're ready to learn the basic figures. For the hour or two you invest in learning the fundamentals you will have hundreds of hours of wholesome fun and enjoyment in dancing. No matter where you go,

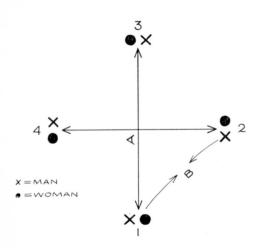

A—Across the hall. The same applies to couples 2 and 4.

B—Corners; same applies to rest of square.

X = MAN
● = WOMAN

Figure 14.   *A Square.*

you will be able to participate successfully.

If you want to dance the whole evening through and come out refreshed instead of worn out, use a light shuffle step (sliding the feet along the floor in a light, easy walk). Avoid skipping, running, or rushing throughout a dance. Know the figures, anticipate the action, and go at it as though you have all the time in the world—and you have.

The square dance is generally made up of three parts: (a) an introduction that involves all couples in the square, (b) a figure that may be of various types but usually does not involve all couples at one time, and (c) an ending that involves the whole square and changes the pace from the figure. Any 2/4 or 4/4 reel tune is usable for accompanying square dance, with the exception of singing calls. There are a wealth of good recordings both with and without calls for the patter type of square dance as well as for the singing type. A selected list of records available for square dancing follows this section. The records that are listed with individual dance descriptions are those that require a specific tune.

BASIC SQUARE DANCE FIGURES

1. HONOR YOUR PARTNER, OR CORNER

Ladies step backward on the right foot (to partner) or left foot (to corner), bending the knee and extending the right foot forward (bow). Gents bend forward from hips. Gent holds lady's left hand in his right as he honors.

2. SWING

Partners take social dance position but step to their own left so that their right sides are together. They may either walk, pivoting in place, or use a buzz step, which is a small, smooth gallop. In either case, you both lead with the right foot. The buzz step is a long step on the right foot and a short step on the left. The feet and hips should be close together and the shoulders lean away. This will increase the centripetal force of the swing.

3. PROMENADE

The gent takes the lady in either the Varsouvianna position or the skater's position (see page 79) and walks around the square, stopping at his home position.

4. BALANCE

Partners take two steps backing away from each other and two steps going toward each other. Another type of balance more characteristic

Swing.

of European folk dance is to step left and swing the right foot across
the left; step right, swing the left foot across the right.

5. DOS-A-DOS

Two people walk toward each other, pass by the right shoulder, step
sideward to the right, and return to position walking backward, passing
left shoulders.

6. CIRCLE LEFT AND RIGHT

All dancers in the square join hands with those on each side of them,
turn slightly left, and walk in that direction; turn to the right and walk
in that direction.

7. FORWARD AND BACK

Take four steps forward and return to place by moving backward (also
called *fall back*).

8. ALLEMANDE LEFT

Face your corner, join left hands, walk around each other, drop hands, and return to place.

9. GRAND RIGHT AND LEFT

All four couples face partners and shake hands. Walk in the direction you are facing, passing your partner and dropping her right hand; meet the next lady and shake left hands; pass her, meet the next with the right, the next with the left, and so forth; continue until you meet your own partner at home. Many calls say, "Meet your partner and promenade." This means that when you meet your partner on the opposite side of the square, you place her on your right and promenade her home. In grand right and left, the gents travel counterclockwise and the ladies go clockwise.

10. PASS THROUGH

Two couples face each other, go between the opposite couple, passing right shoulders with the person you are facing.

11. RIGHT AND LEFT THROUGH

Two couples face each other and pass through, passing right shoulders with the person you face. The gent takes his partner's left hand in his left, places his right arm around her waist, and turns her in place counterclockwise (gent pivots backward and lady pivots forward).

12. LADIES CHANGE OR CHAIN

Two couples face each other. The two ladies join right hands, pass each other, drop hands, and give the opposite gent the left hand. The gent places his right arm around the lady's waist and turns her counterclockwise in place. *Change*, or *chain*, *right back* means that you repeat the figure to get back to your partner.

13. SASHAY

A slide step sideward (see page 11).

Right and Left Through. "Pass through the opposite couple."

Right and Left Through. "Turn in place."

Ladies Change or Chain.

14. DOCEY-DOE

Two couples face each other. Join hands and circle halfway round; pass through (as in Number 10) and face partner. The gent takes his partner's left hand, turns her around counterclockwise until she faces the opposite gent. Drop your partner and take the opposite lady with the right hand and turn her around clockwise until she is facing her partner and you are facing yours; drop her and take your partner with the left hand; place the right hand around her waist and turn counterclockwise in place (gent pivoting backward and lady forward).

15. STAR

Two couples turn right shoulders to center and place right hand on wrist of person ahead. Walk CW. Reverse, and place left hand in center and walk CC.

ARMY AND NAVY SQUARE [5]

Record: MacGregor 614-B.
Tune: *Solomon Levi* (without calls)

Call	Directions

INTRODUCTION

It's all join hands and circle,	Join hands, walk CW.
You circle left hands round.	
Now, the other way back, you're going wrong;	Change direction, walk CC.
You circle to the right.	
Now, everybody, swing your gal,	Swing your partner.
You swing her up and down,	
And when you get through swinging her, you promenade around.	Walk partner around square to starting position.
The first couple back to back,	Couple 1 turns back to back, walks around outside of square, salute partner as you pass, meet at home.
You march around the ring,	
Salute your partners halfway round, and keep right in the swing.	
You walk right by your partners,	Pass your partner, salute corner,
Salute your corners all,	
And turn and swing your partner round, and promenade the hall.	Swing your partner, Promenade.

---

[5] International Square and Folk Dance Festival, Canton, N.Y., 1951. Sponsored by St. Laurence University.

Note: The figure is then repeated for second, third, and fourth couples. Then repeat for side couples (#2 and #4) and head couples (#1 and #3); then all four couples repeat the figure at the same time.

STAR BY THE RIGHT [6]

Call	Directions

INTRODUCTION

Honors right and honors left.	Bow to partner, then corner.
All join hands and circle left.	Join hands, circle CW.
Break and swing and promenade back.	Swing partner, promenade home.

FIGURE

First couple out to the couple on the right,	Couple 1 goes out to couple 2.
* Form a star with the right hand crossed.	All place R hand up in center, hold the wrist of the person in front of you, walk CW.
Back with the left, and don't get lost.	Reverse direction, place left hand in center, and walk CC.
Swing your opposite with the right,	One-hand swing with right hand to corner or opposite.
Now your partner with your left,	Swing partner with left—one-hand swing.
And on to the next.	Go on to couple 3.

Repeat twice from *, changing last line to:

Balance home.

ENDING

And everybody swing.	Swing your partner.
Now swing the left-hand lady with the left hand;	Allemande left.
Right to your partner and a right and left grand.	Grand right and left.
Promenade eight when you come straight.	Promenade home.

---

[6] From *Cowboy Dances*, by Lloyd Shaw. Caldwell, Idaho: The Caxton Printers, Ltd., 1939, p. 167. Used by special permission of the copyright owners.

SIOUX CITY SUE (singing call)   Record: Imperial 1099

Call   Directions

INTRODUCTION

Swing, boys, swing; everybody swing,   Swing your partner.
Swing your honey 'round and 'round.
Promenade around the town.   Promenade.
Promenade with her, she'll promenade with
  you,
And when you get her home, boys, you swing   Swing partner.
  Sioux City Sue.

FIGURE

First couple to the right, you circle four   Couple 1 moves to couple 2, joins hands,
  hands 'round.   circles left.
* Now dos-a-dos your opposite,   Pass around each other back to back
The sweetest girl in town.   (with opposite).
Dos-a-dos your own girl,   Dos-a-dos partners.
She'll dos-a-dos with you.
Then take her in your arms, boy,
And swing Sioux City Sue.   Swing partner.
On to the next, you circle four hands round.   Travel to couple 3.

Repeat from * twice.

RED RIVER VALLEY (singing call)   Record: Old Timer 8001

Call   Directions

INTRODUCTION

Now, it's allemande left on the corner,   Allemande left.
And you grand right and left half around.   Grand right and left.
When you meet your own, you will prome-
  nade her home,   Meet partner, promenade.
And swing with your Red River gal.   Swing partner.

FIGURE

First couple to the right and you balance;	Couple 1 goes to #2, balance.
Then you circle to the left and to the right.	Join hands, circle L and R.
Then you swing with the girl in the valley;	Swing your opposite.
Then you swing with your Red River girl.	Swing partner.
* Then it's on to the next and you balance;	Couple 1 goes to #3, balance.
Then you circle to the left and to the right.	Join hands, circle L and R.
Then you swing with the girl in the valley;	Swing with opposite.
Then you swing with your Red River gal.	Swing partner.

Repeat from *.
Then start from introduction, following with
    couple 2; then over again for #3 and #4.

DIVE FOR THE OYSTER [7]

Call	*Directions*

INTRODUCTION

All jump up and never come down.	Jump, swing partners.
Swing your honey around and around,	
'Til the hollow of your foot makes a hole in the ground,	
And promenade, boys, promenade.	Promenade.

FIGURE

First couple out to the couple on the right,	Couple 1 goes out to face #2.
* And dive for the oyster.	Join hands, circle L, couple 1 dives under raised arms of #2 and comes back again.
Dive for the clam,	Couple 2 dives under arms of #1 and back again.
Dive for the sardine and take a full can.	Couple 1 dives through #2 turning back to back, pulling #2 through. Couple 2 turns face to face and under own arms when through.
Four hands up, and here we go,	
Round and round with a docey-doe,	Circle left, docey-doe.
And on to the next.	

---

7 *Ibid.*, p. 197. Used by special permission of the copyright owners.

Repeat twice from °, changing last line to:
  Balance home.

Repeat whole dance for couples 2, 3 and 4.

ENDING

Call	Directions
And everybody swing.	Swing partner.
Now allemande left with your left hand,	Allemande left.
Right to your partner and a right and left grand.	Grand right and left.
Promenade eight when you come straight.	Promenade.

FORWARD SIX, FALL BACK SIX [8]

Call   Directions

INTRODUCTION

Honor your partner and the lady by your side.	Bow to partner and corner.
All join hands and circle wide.	Join hands, circle L.
Break and swing and promenade home.	Swing partner, promenade.

FIGURE

First couple out to the couple on the right.	Couple 1 goes to couple 2.
Circle four; leave that girl, go on to the next.	Leave lady #1, go to next couple alone.
Circle three; take that girl on to the next, circle four.	Circle with couple 3; take lady #3 on to couple 4.
Leave that girl and go home alone.	Leave lady #3 and go home alone (formation is now two lines of three and two single gents).
° Forward six and fall back six;	Two lines of three go forward and back
Forward two and fall back two;	Two single gents go forward and back
Forward six and pass right through;	Two lines of three pass through each other and turn around.
Forward two and pass right through.	Two single gents pass and change places.

Repeat from °.

---

8 *Ibid.*, pp. 67-68. Used by special permission of the copyright owners.

ENDING

Swing your corner like a swingin' on a gate,	Swing corner.
And now your partner, if you're not too late.	Swing partner.
Now allemande left with your left hand,	Allemande left.
And right to your partner and a right and left grand.	Grand right and left.
And promenade eight when you come straight.	Promenade.

Repeat whole dance, starting with couple 2, and then with couples 3 and 4.

INSIDE ARCH [9]   *Record with calls:* Old Timer 8019

Call   *Directions*

INTRODUCTION

All eight balance, all eight swing.	Balance to partner and swing.
* Left allemande and a right-hand grand,	Left allemande, grand right and left.
And promenade, oh, promenade.	Promenade.

FIGURE

First couple out to the couple on the right,	Couple 1 goes to couple 2
With a four and a half.	Join hands, circle ½ CW.
Inside arch and outside under;	Couple 1 (inside) raise inside joined hands; couple 2 goes under and into
Inside arch and outside under;	circle straight across to couple 4, while
Inside arch and outside under.	#1 turns to face center (lady on right). Couple 2 arches and #4 goes under and across; #4 arches and #1 goes under; couple 1 arches and #2 goes under (couple 1 is now in position of #4; #4 is in position of #2; #2 is in center).
Now circle four with the odd couple, oh.	Couple 2 circles with couple 3.
Around and around and a docey-doe,	Docey-doe.
And on to the next with a four and a half.	Couple 2 goes to couple 4 and circles half around.
Inside arch and outside under;	
Inside arch and outside under;	
Inside arch and outside under;	(Same as explanation above.)
Inside arch and outside under.	

---

[9] *Ibid.*, pp. 341-342. Used by special permission of the copyright owners.

ENDING

Balance home and swing 'em all night.
Allemande left, go left and right.
Hand over hand around the ring;
Hand over hand with the dear little thing.
Meet your partner and promenade.

All eight swing.
Allemande left; grand right and left.

Promenade home.

SPLIT THE RING [10]

Call   *Directions*

INTRODUCTION

Salute your company and the lady on your left.	Bow to partner and corner.
All join hands and circle to the left.	Circle left.
Break and swing and promenade back.	Swing partner, promenade.

FIGURE

First couple balance, first couple swing.	Couple 1 balance and swing.
Go down the center and split the ring.	Go down and cut between couple 3.
The lady goes right and the gent goes left.	Lady goes around outside of set CW and gent CC.
Swing when you meet both head and feet,	When back to place, couples 1 and 3 swing partners.
And the side four the same.	Couples 2 and 4 swing partners.
Left allemande the corner girl,	All allemande L.
And swing your own with another whirl.	Swing partner.
Now down the center as you did before;	Couple 1 goes down center; lady cuts
Down the center and cast off four.	between couples 2 and 3, and gent between #3 and #4, and back to place.
Swing when you meet at the head and the feet,	Couples 1 and 3 swing partner.
And the side four the same.	Couples 2 and 4 swing.
Down to center as you used to do;	Couple 1 down center again.
Down the center and cast off two.	Lady cuts between couple 2; gent cuts between couple 4.
Swing when you meet both the head and the feet.	Everybody swing.

ENDING

Allemande left with your left hand.	Allemande left.
Right hand to partner and a grand right and left.	Grand right and left.
Promenade eight when you come straight.	Meet your partner, promenade.

---

[10] *Ibid.*, p. 288. Used by special permission of the copyright owners.

FORWARD SIX, FALL BACK EIGHT [11]

Call	Directions
INTRODUCTION	
Swing your partners, don't be late.	Swing partners.
Swing your corner like swingin' on a gate.	Swing corners.
Now your own, and promenade eight.	Swing partner, promenade.
FIGURE	
First couple balance and swing.	Step away from partner, toward partner, and swing.
Down the center and split the the ring.	Couple 1 goes between couple 3.
Lady goes right and the gent goes left,	Lady goes around gent and stands beside him; gent goes around lady and stands beside her. (All four are in a line.)
And four in line you stand.	
Forward four fall back four.	Line of four goes into center four steps and back again; gent of couple 1 leads line to his right with slide step sideward stopping behind couple 4.
Sashay four to the right.	
Forward six and fall back eight.	Ends of line of four join hands with couple 4; all six go forward four steps; fall back four with couple 2 coming along.
Forward eight and fall back six.	All eight go forward (couple 1 backward); couple 1 stays in place as the six go back again.
Sashay four to the right.	Original group of four slides around to couple 1's position.
Forward four and fall back four.	Four take four steps forward and back.
Sashay four to the right.	Four slide right in back of couple 2.
Forward six, fall back eight.	(As explained above.)
Forward eight and fall back six.	(As explained above.)
Sashay four to the right.	Group of four slides right to original position.
Forward four and fall back four.	(As before.)
Forward four and circle four.	Go forward, join hands in circle.
Ladies doe and gents you know.	Two ladies dos-a-dos and two gents dos-a-dos.
Circle again and docey-doe.	Circle, docey-doe.
ENDING	
Balance home, and everybody swing.	Return home, balance with partner, and everybody swing.
Left allemande and a right-hand grand.	(See page 63.)
Meet your partner, promenade.	Promenade.

---

[11] *Ibid.*, p. 261. Used by special permission of the copyright owners.

/J. M. HODGES LIBRARY
WHARTON COUNTY JUNIOR COLLEGE
WHARTON, TEXAS

RIGHT AND LEFT THROUGH

Call	*Directions*

INTRODUCTION

Salute your partner and the lady on the left.	Bow to partner, corner.
All poin hands and circle to the left.	All eight join hands, circle CW.
Break and swing and promenade home.	Swing partner, promenade.

FIGURE

First and third couples lead to the right,	Couples 1 and 3 to #2 and #4.
With a right and left through,	(See page 63.)
And a right and left back.	Right and left through.
Two ladies change and change right back.	(See page 63.) Ladies change.
Circle four, and 'round you go,	Couples 1 and 2, 3 and 4 circle left.
Break that ring with a docey-doe.	(See page 63.)
Dough, dough, a little more dough,	
Chicken in the bread pan pecking at dough,	(Patter.)
One more doe, and on you go.	Go home.

ENDING

Balance home and swing 'em all 'round,	Balance and swing partner.
Left to your corner as you come down,	Allemande left.
Grand right and left all around,	Grand right and left.
Meet your own and promenade.	Promenade partner.

RIGHT HAND HIGH, LEFT LADY UNDER

Call	*Directions*

INTRODUCTION

Grab your partners and swing 'em around.	Swing partner.
With one foot up, the other foot down.	
Allemande left with a grand right and left,	Allemande left, grand right and left.
Promenade, boys, promenade.	Promenade.

FIGURE

First couple out to the couple on the right.	Couple 1 goes to couple 2.
Circle four with all your might.	Join hands, circle CW.
Leave that lady where she be, and on to the next; you circle 3.	Leave lady #1. Circle with couple 3.

Steal that lady like honey from a bee,
On to the next, and circle four.
Leave that girl, go home alone.
* It's six to the center, and back you go,
Two gents loop with a dos-a-dos,
Right lady high, left lady under,

Form new three's, and don't be slow.

Take lady #3 along.
Circle with couple 4.
Leave lady #3, go home.
Two lines of three go to center and back.
Gents #1 and #3 dos-a-dos.
In lines of three; gent raises R hand, pulls ladies toward each other, passing them; left lady goes under gent's right arm while right lady passes to left side of gent. Ladies go to head and foot, making lines of three with the end gents.

Repeat from * three times.

ENDING

Everybody forward and back.
Girls to the center and ring to the left.
Gents join hands and circle right.
Weave that basket, circle left.

Weave that basket the other way,

Feel her heft, boys, what does she weigh?
Now break and swing and promenade home.

All eight into circle and back.
Ladies circle CW.
Gents circle CC.
Ladies raise arms and loop around gents' shoulders; circle CW.
Ladies unloop and gents raise arms over ladies' heads to inside of circle.
Patter.
Swing partner, promenade.

Repeat whole dance for couples 2, 3, and 4.

SELECTED RECORDS FOR SQUARE DANCING

Black Mountain 102 *Up Jumped the Devil* (Instrumental)
Tennessee Wagoner (Instrumental)
110 *Arkansas Traveler* (Instrumental)
Dance Around Molly (Instrumental)
127 *Sugar Foot Rag* (Instrumental)
108 *Whirlpool Square* (with calls—Gotcher)
Tunnel Through (with calls—Gotcher)

Black Mountain 133 *Shiek of Araby* (with singing calls—Van Antwerp)
Simplicity Hash (with singing calls—Van Antwerp)
Capitol 79-40162 *Skip to My Lou, Arkansas Traveler*
Cumberland Gap — Fox and Hounds
79-40202 *Chinese Breakdown— Ocean Waves*
79-40160 *Leather Britches, Turkey in the Straw, Tennessee Wagoner, Back up and Push*

Capitol 79-40161 *Down Yonder, Buffalo Gals, Devil's Dream, Old Joe Clark*

Columbia-English DX 1245 *Arcadian Lancers, Fig. 1 and 3*

DX 1246 *Arcadian Lancers, Fig. 5 St. Bernard Waltz*

Folkraft   1136 *Alabama Jubilee Around the Corner* (with calls)

1134 *Glory Hallelujah* (with calls) *Lady Around the Lady* (with calls)

1254 *Grapevine Twist* (all calls on one side, instrumental on the other side)

1263 *Jessie Polka Square* (same)

1273 *Sashay Partners* (same)

1280 *Spanish Cavaliers* (same)

1256 *Texas Star* (same)

1243 *Portland Fancy* (with calls)

1249 *Virginia Reel* (calls on both sides—simple version)

1285 *Northern Lights* (with calls —Parker)

Imperial Album FD-36 (78) *Square Dances* (with calls—Smith) A1-FD-8 *Square Dances* (with calls—Smith)

Lloyd Shaw *Singing Quadrilles—Album 5* (with Instructions)

133 *Dos-a-Dos your Corners All*

134 *First Couple Down Center*

135 *Little Old Log Cabin*

136 *Waltz that Girl Behind You*

137 *The Flower Girl Waltz*

138 *The Flower Girl Waltz*

139 *The Wearin' o' the Green*

140 *The Old Waltz Quadrille*

x59 *Hi Lili* (Instrumental—instructions included)

x60 *Hi Lili* (called by Lloyd Shaw)

MacGregor   636 *Chinese Breakdown*

662 *Down Yonder*

670 *Golden Slippers*

688 *Blue Tail Fly* (with calls —Jones)

659 *California, Here I Come* (with calls—Jones)

659 *Crawdad Song* (with calls —Jones)

001-4 *Hot Time in the Old Town Tonight* (with calls— Gotcher)

006-1 *Cats Miaow* (with calls —Hoheisal)

675 *Couple Elbow Swing* (with calls—Holden)

657 *Hurry, Hurry, Hurry— Jessie Polka Square*

Old Timer 8030 *San Antonio Rose* (with calls—Nelson) *Hot Time in the Old Town Tonight* (with calls—Nelson)

8001 *Red River Valley Varsoviana*

Windsor 7412 *My Pretty Girl* (with calls— Johnson) *Marching Through Georgia*

7401 *Beginners' Practice Dances* (with calls—Alumbaugh). Sides A and B

7407 *Mañana* (with calls—Johnson) *Same Old Shillelagh* (with calls—Alumbaugh)

7122 *Down South* (call sheet included for singing calls) *Put on Your Old Gray Bonnet* (call sheet included for singing calls)

SELECTED SOURCES FOR SQUARE DANCING

Bol, Lawrence, ed., *The Square Dance.* Chicago: Best Advertising Service, 1950. (Includes mixers and rounds.)

Bossing, Edward, *Handbook of Favorite Dances.* Chicago: Fitzsimmons, 1955.

Chase, Ann Hastings, *The Singing Caller.* New York: Association Press, 1944.

Colby, Fred W., *Square Dances—Tennessee Style.* Knoxville: The University of Tennessee, College of Agriculture, 1953.

Czarnowski, Lucile K., *Dances of Early California Days.* Palo Alto, Cal.: Pacific Books, 1950.

Damon, Samuel Foster, *The History of Square Dancing.* Worcester, Mass.: American Antiquarian Society, 1952.

Day, Mel, and Jere Long, *In Idaho it's Docey-Doe.* Boise, Idaho: Mel Day, 1920; Longmont, 1950.

Durlacher, Ed., *Honor Your Partner.* New York: Devin-Adair Co., 1949.

Eisenberg, Helen, and Larry Eisenberg, *And Promenade All.* Nashville: The Methodist Publishing House, 1947.

Eisenberg, Larry, *The World of Fun Series.* Nashville: The Methodist Publishing House, 1951.

Ford, Henry, *Good Morning,* 4th ed. Dearborn, Michigan: 1943.

Gowing, Gene, *The Square Dancer's Guide.* New York: Crown Publishing Co., 1957.

Greggerson, Herb F., *Herb's Blue Bonnet Calls.* El Paso, Texas: H. F. Greggerson, Jr., Box 3061, Station A, 1940, 1948.

Holden, Rickey, *The Contra Dance Book.* Newark, N. J.: American Squares, 1956.

————, *The Square Dance Caller.* Newark, N. J.: American Squares, 1951.

Hunt, Paul, and Charlotte Underwood, *Calico Rounds; Round and Folk Dance Teacher.* New York: Harper & Brothers, 1955.

Kraus, Richard G., *Square Dances of Today and How to Teach and Call Them:* New York: Ronald Press, 1950.

Mainey, F., *The Old Time Dancers Handbook.* London: Jenkins, 1953.

Mayo, Margot, *The American Square Dance.* New York: Sentinel Books, 1943.

Osgood, Bob, *Square Dancing for Intermediates.* Los Angeles, California: Sets in Order, 1950.

————, *Square Dancing, the Newer and Advanced.* Los Angeles, California: Sets in Order, 1951.

————, and Jack Hoheisal, *Square Dancing for Beginners.* Los Angeles 48, California. Sets in Order, 1949.

Owens, Lee, *Advanced Square Dance Figures of the West and Southwest.* Palo Alto, Cal.: Pacific Books, 1950.

————, *American Square Dances of the West and Southwest.* Palo Alto, Cal.: Pacific Books, 1949.

Shaw, Lloyd, *Cowboy Dances.* Caldwell, Idaho: Caxton Printers, 1939.

Smith, Frank H., *The Appalachian Square Dance.* Berea, Ky.: Berea College, 1955.

Smith, Raymond, *Collection of Square Dances and Mixers,* Supplement to *Square Dance Handbook,* 2nd ed. Dallas, Texas: Raymond Smith, 1950.

————, *Square Dance Handbook,* Vol. I. Dallas, Texas: Raymond Smith, 1947.

Tolman, Beth, and Ralph Page, *The Country Dance Book.* Weston, Vt.: The Countryman Press, 1937.

CHAPTER VI

Round Dance (American)

On the heels of the revival of the square dance came that of the old-time round dances that were done when grandmother was a girl. These old-time dances are mainly couple dances that are done to a specific piece of music and travel around the room. In recent years, many new round dances have been created by active dance groups in various parts of the country. Those that meet with wide acceptance will also become part of the heritage of American Round Dance. These are the American folk dances that bear a closer resemblance to the European folk dances. They are based on several steps that have come to be known as basic steps for folk dancing of all types.

These basic steps will be presented first. You will do well to learn these steps before trying the dances. Once you know the basic steps used, you will catch on to almost any dance very easily.

Basic Steps

TWO-STEP 2/4 OR 4/4

The two-step may be done sideward, forward, or turning. In round dancing, it is more often used in a forward and turning direction. For abbreviation symbols and their meaning, see page 30.

Pattern	*Rhythm*
Step fwd L	Q 1
Cl R to L	Q &
Step fwd L	S 2

Repeat, starting R.

$\frac{2}{4}$ ♪♪ ♩ |

I   and   2

S   CL   S

$\frac{4}{4}$ ♩ ♩ ♩ ♩ |

1   2   3   4

S   CL   S   Hd

Note: This step-close-step pattern is used in turning in closed position by taking it sideward and pivoting ½ turn on the last step. It then takes two two-steps to complete a full turn. The two-step may be done as it is described here, or the first step may be sideward (side-close-side, or side-close-forward). The sideward step is more easily used for turning.

Skater's Position.

"Shoulder or Varsouvianna Position."

POLKA 2/4 OR 6/8

The polka step follows the two-step because it is so similar to it. In order to make a polka out of a two-step, you simply add a short hop after the completed two-step. The rhythm is uneven.

You pause on the end of the two-step before hopping (see the fundamental locomotor steps, page 11). The difference between the 2/4 and 6/8 polka is that the latter is slower and has more of a lilting quality; there is time to go higher into the air on the hop.

Pattern	Rhythm
Step fwd L	Q 1
Cl R to L	Q &
Step fwd L	S 2
Hop L	q a
Repeat, starting R.	

1 and 2 a
S CL S H

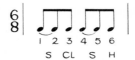

1 2 3 4 5 6
S CL S H

The easiest way to catch on to a polka step if you don't know a two-step is to slide or gallop (see the fundamental steps, page 11) to the left eight times, to the right eight times, to the left four times, right four times, left twice, right twice, and keep repeating the two's. When you get down to the two left and right, you are doing a polka sideward; keep doing it until you know it thoroughly enough to do the same step forward. After you master this, try it turning. You may also continue moving in the same direction in the circle by facing alternately inward and outward rather than changing the direction of movement.

"Shoulder-Waist Position."

SCHOTTISCHE 4/4

The schottische step is very similar to both the two-step and the polka. There is just one small difference between the polka and schottische, but it makes the quality of the step very different from that of the polka. You have noticed that the hop in the polka is a very short or quick one—a fraction of a second before beginning the step again. In the schottische, the hop gets the full beat. This makes the step-close-step-hop all even in time.

$$\frac{4}{4} \quad \text{♩ ♩ ♩ ♩}$$

I   2   3   4

S CL S H

Pattern	Rhythm
Step fwd L	Q 1
Step fwd R (or Cl R to L)	Q 2
Step fwd L	Q 3
Hop L	Q 4
Repeat, starting R.	

MAZURKA 3/4

The mazurka step is one that is rarely seen on the American dance floor in its original form. It has survived in modified form, however, as is evident in the very popular dance, the Varsouvianna. The mazurka has distinct characteristics that belong to no other step. Although it exists in 3/4 time, the second beat is accented. The second step is not only a close, but a cut step in which the left leg is kicked forward. On the hop, the free leg is brushed backward across the hopping leg.

Pattern	Rhythm
Step diagonally fwd L.	Q 1
Cl R to L, kicking L diagonally fwd.	Q 2
Hop R and bring L foot across R.	Q 3

Repeat consecutively on same side.

$$\frac{3}{4} \quad \text{♩ ♩ ♩}$$

I   2   3

S CL H

WALTZ 3/4

The waltz step is the basis for one of the most beautiful forms of round dancing. It also seems to be the most difficult for young people to learn. It is entirely even, and the weight must be shifted with each step. The step alternates from one side to another.

Pattern	Rhythm
Step fwd L	Q 1
Step sdwd R	Q 2
Cl L to R	Q 3
Repeat, starting R.	

For waltz turning, see page 46.

Popular Round Dances

Now that you know the basic steps, try making use of them in the following selection of popular round dances. It is necessary to memorize the step sequences in round dances before you can dance them. They are set to music and do not give you the freedom that you find in square dancing. The better you learn these dances, the more you will enjoy dancing them. Listen to your music first, and, as you figure out step patterns, do them to the music.

TEN PRETTY GIRLS

Records: Folkraft 1036
Methodist 113
MacGregor 604

Partners stand side by side facing the same direction. Place arms around each other's waist. You may join two couples together or any number of couples. This dance is done in a line traveling around the room. Everyone starts with the left foot. For abbreviations and their meaning, see page 30. The counts required for step patterns appear in parentheses following the steps.

Fig. 1. Reach fwd with the L heel (1-2).
Touch L toe behind R heel (3-4).
Step L in place, step sdwd R, Cl L to R (5-7, hold 8).
Repeat the above, starting R.

Fig. 2. Walk fwd four slow steps (1-8).
Swing L foot fwd (1-2).
Swing L foot bkwd (3-4).
Stamp 3 times in place, L, R, L (5-7, hold 8).
Start from beginning with R foot.

TETON MOUNTAIN STOMP   *Record:* Windsor 7615

This dance was adapted from the Buffalo Glide by Doc Alumbaugh. A circle of couples must be in closed position (see page 24), with each gent's left shoulder toward the center of the circle. This dance should be done with a gay and bouncy spirit.

Fig. 1. Moving toward center, step sdwd L, Cl R to L, step sdwd L, and stamp R (1-4).
Repeat, starting R, and going away from center.
Step L in place, stamp R (1-2).
Step R in place, stamp L (3-4), and change to left open reverse position (see page 26).
Walk four steps fwd, L, R, L, R (1-4) and change to right open reverse position.*

Fig. 2. Walk four steps in line of direction (CC), L,R, L, R (1-4), with gent traveling backward. Change back to left open reverse position.
Walk four steps in line of direction (CC).
Two two-steps, turning in closed position, L, R,L, R,L,R (1-8).
Pivot in place in closed position, L,R,L,R.

---

* Change to right open reverse position by pivoting in place one-half turn. Lady now faces forward (CC) and gent backward (CW).

COTTON EYED JOE

Record: MacGregor 604
Paramount 1008
Imperial 1045

Cotton Eyed Joe can be done as a graceful dance or it can be a dance of vigor and character of Cotton Eyed Joe. Regardless of whether it is done with the stamping and crude twist or the polite and social form, it is an interesting dance. From the name itself you can gather a picture of this character. Pointed toes and soft movement would not describe him well. You will find many variations to this dance. This variation is a very simple one.

Couples are scattered on the floor in regular open position. The gent begins left and the lady right. The gent's part is described. The lady does the opposite except when specifically noted.

FIG. 1. Extend L heel sdwd (1-2).
Cross L toe over R (3-4).
Stamp in place 3 times (1-3, hold 4).
Repeat, starting R.

FIG. 2. Circle away from partner—lady CW, gent CC, with: 6 heel-toe steps (place weight on heel and come down on toe) (1-12).
3 stamps in place (1-3, hold 4), bringing feet up high.

FIG. 3. Chug step to the L 4 times (place weight on L; shift weight momentarily to R just long enough to push sdwd L, keeping foot in contact with floor).
Repeat three times in succession.

Chug step to the R 4 times.

FIG. 4. Two-step four times, turning CW and traveling CC in circle.

Note: Figure 2 can be used to improvise any wild movements you want to do. In the polite form, this part consists of four two-steps away from partner.

JESSIE POLKA

Record: Capitol 10251
MacGregor 617

Any number of dancers may do this dance together, as it is done in a line formation moving around the room. All dancers face the same direction side by side and place their arms around the waists of the persons on either side. This dance is also done by hooking elbows. Everyone starts on the same foot and does the same steps.

FIG. 1. Place L heel fwd with no weight (1).
Bring L foot to R and take weight (2).
Reach bkwd with R toe—no weight (3).
Bring R foot to L—no weight (4).
Place R heel fwd—no weight (5).
Bring R to L and take weight (6).
Place L heel fwd—no weight (7).
Cross L toe in front of R—no weight (8).

FIG. 2. Four polka steps (see page 12) fwd (1-8).

When the foot is reaching forward, the body should tilt backward; when reaching backward, the body should tilt forward. After the sequence of weight-shifting is conquered, keep a constant hop going on the foot that has the weight. Whenever the left foot is doing the figure, the right is hopping; just the reverse when the right foot is doing the figure.

ARIZONA POLKA

Record: Kismet 140
Victor 25-1009
Windsor 7624

Couples are in a circle in shoulder position (see page 80); both start with the same foot. Gent's part is described. Lady does the opposite except when specifically noted.

FIG. 1. Extend L heel diagonally fwd; bring L toe across R (1-2).
Gent: Take 3 steps in place, L,R,L (3 and 4).
Lady: Take 3 steps, crossing to gent's L side (3 and 4).
Repeat, starting R.

FIG. 2. Extend L heel and cross R, as in Fig. 1 (1-2).
Gent: Drop L hand and take 3 steps in place, L,R,L (3 and 4).
Lady: Take 3 steps turning ½ CW (3 and 4).
Repeat, starting R.

FIG. 3. Two two-steps fwd (1 and 2, 3 and 4).
Gent: Releases L hand, takes two two-steps fwd again, but
not traveling as far (1 and 2, 3 and 4).
Lady: Turns under gent's R arm CW with two two-steps (1 and
2, 3 and 4).

HEEL AND TOE POLKA

Record: Windsor 7624
Victor 25-1009

Couples are scattered about the room   Gent starts left and lady starts right.
in closed position, using an elbow hold.

FIG. 1. Extend L heel L sdwd and cross L toe over R (1-2).
Polka * step L (3-4).
Extend R heel R sdwd and cross R toe over L (1-2).
Polka step R(3-4).

FIG. 2. Four polka steps around the room (1-8).

FIG. 3. Variations to be substituted for Figure 1:
Dos-a-dos ** your partner with four polkas, starting diagonally
fwd L for gent and diagonally fwd R for the lady.
Point L foot sdwd, Cl L to R, and repeat (1-4).
Four slide steps L sdwd (1-4).
Repeat all, starting R (1-8).

SCHOTTISCHE (Progressive)

Record: Imperial 1046

Couples are in a circle in shoulder   the same foot.
position. The gent and lady start with

FIG. 1. Point L toe diagonally sdwd L (1-2).
Cross L toe over R (3-4).
Gent: Drop R hands; take one schottische step in place (1-4).
Lady: One schottische step, circling in front of gent ½ turn CC.
Point R toe diagonally sdwd R (1-2).
Cross R toe over L (3-4).
Gent: One schottische in place (1-4).
Lady: One schottische, turning ½ CC under gent's R arm, end-
ing in starting position.

---

* See page 12.
** See page 62.

FIG. 2. Basic Schottische step forward with chorus:
Step fwd L, Cl R to L, step fwd L, hop L (1-4).
Repeat, starting R.
Step L, hop L, step R, hop R (1-4).
Step L, hop L, step R, hop R (1-4).

Note: This may be used as a mixer by changing as follows: On the last part of Figure 1, the lady goes to the gent behind her partner on the schottische step instead of circling back to place beside her partner.

TENNESSEE WIG WALK

Record: King 1237
Decca 28846

Couples are in a single circle, with men facing CC and women CW. Partners hold right hands.

FIG. 1. Point L foot in front of R twice (1-2,3-4).
Cross L in back of R, step R sdwd, cross L in front of R (1,2,3-4).
Join L hands.
Repeat, starting with R foot.

FIG. 2. Join R hands and make one turn CW, stepping L,R,L, and brush or scuff the R foot (1,2,3,4).
Continue CW, stepping R,L,R, brush L (1,2,3,4).
Release partner's hand. Woman travels CW, man CC. All walk 3 steps fwd. Clap hands of girl you meet.
Walk 3 steps fwd again, and take that person for new partner.

VARSOUVIANNA

Record: Shaw 103
Windsor 7615

This dance is practically the only one of the old-time dances based on a Mazurka step that is surviving today. Actually, the step is not a true Mazurka but a simplification of one. Its origin is unknown, but many claims exist and they all differ considerably. The characteristic of the Mazurka step is that the second beat is accented and it begins on count 3 of a ¾ measure. For the Mazurka step, see pages 12 and 82.

Couples are in shoulder position. The gent and the lady may use either the same foot or the opposite foot.

Fig. 1. Brush the L foot diagonally across the R (3).
Step fwd L, Cl R to L (1-2)
Repeat all.
Brush L foot diagonally across R (3).
Step fwd L, Cl R to L (1-2).
Step L, point R toe diagonally fwd R (3, 1-2).

Repeat from beginning, starting R.

Fig. 2. Brush L foot across R (3).
Gent: Step back of R with L, pivot ⅛ turn CW (1).
Step R, in place step L, point R (2-3, 1 hold 2-3).
Repeat this figure three times.

Fig. 3. Waltz 8 times around the room.

Note: Some recordings allow for the waltz figures and some don't. You must listen to know. Some recordings are also made to repeat Figure 1. There are many recordings of this tune—more popularly known as "Put Your Little Foot."

CHAPANECAS

Record: MacGregor 608
Folk Dancer MH 1016

Couples are in a circle facing each other, with the gent on the inside with his back to the center of the circle. The origin of this dance is unknown. It is a favorite Mexican folk tune that has been used by many people. However, the dance is very much American in character and makeup. The gent begins right and the lady left. Both hands are joined across.

Fig. 1. Step L sdwd, swing R foot across L (1-3).
Step R sdwd, swing L foot across R (1-3).
Step L sdwd, pivot 1 full turn away from partner (1-2).
Stamp twice in place as you clap twice (3-1, hold 2-3).
Repeat, starting R.

Fig. 2. With hands joined across—
Step away from partner (bkwd) (1-3).
Step toward partner (fwd) (1-3).
Step away again (1-2).
Clap twice (3-1, hold 2-3).
Repeat the figure, starting with step toward partner; on two claps, place arms around partner and clap behind each other.

Fig. 3. Waltz your partner 14 waltzes around the room, turning her under gent's R arm on the last two waltzes.

Note: If you cannot waltz well in closed position, practice in conversation position—side by side with the inside hands joined. Your first waltz will be face to face, the second back to back, and so forth.

BLACKHAWK WALTZ   *Record:* Shaw 1-103

Imperial 1006

This dance may be done easily in conversational position, shoulder position, or closed position. It takes on a different look in closed position because the crossing is done forward by the gent and backward by the lady, whose balance is much more difficult in closed position. It is described here in conversation and/or shoulder position. The gent and lady start on the same foot.

FIG. 1. Four waltz balance steps as follows:

Step fwd L, Cl R to L without shifting weight, and hold or pause (1-2, hold 3).

Step bkwd R, Cl L to R without shifting weight, and hold or pause (1-2, hold 3).

Repeat whole figure.

FIG. 2. Cross Waltz *:

Step across in front of R with L foot (1-3).

Step across in front of L with R foot (1-3).

Cross L over R, step sdwd R, Cl L to R, point the R foot diagonally fwd R (1-3, 1 hold 2,3).

Repeat, starting R.

Repeat whole figure.

SELECTED RECORDS FOR ROUND DANCE

The following records are suggestions for further round dancing. In practically all cases, directions for the dance come with the purchase of records.

Lloyd Shaw Album 4 *Learning to Waltz* (complete instructions and development of the waltz). 4 records

Lloyd Shaw 103 *Varsouvianna* (with instructions and spoken cues)
Blackhawk Waltz (same)
105 *Laces and Graces* (same)
Glow Worm Gavotte (same)
109 *Irish Waltz* (same)
Waltz of the Bells (same)

---

* Turn the body to face in each direction specified. Change direction on count three of each step.

Lloyd Shaw 141 *Manitou* (same)
          *The Three-Step (Moon-
               winks)* (same)
          121 *Tucker Waltz*

Lloyd Shaw 122 *Five Feet Two*
RCA Victor 25-1009 *Hot Pretzels*
                   Beer Barrel Polka

SELECTED SOURCES FOR ROUND DANCE

Hamilton, Frank, *The American Round Dance Handbook*. Los Angeles 48, California: Sets in Order, 1957.

Harris, Jane A., Anne Pittman, and Marlys S. Waller, *Dance A While*. Minneapolis, Minn.: Burgess Publishing Co., 1950.

Shaw, Lloyd, *The Round Dance Book*. Caldwell, Idaho: The Caxton Printers, 1950.

CHAPTER VII

Folk Dances of Other Countries

PENNY REEL (British West Indies, Jamaican Calypso)
Choreography by: Winifred Hooper   *Record:* Trojan XX02

The Calypso music that has gained such tremendous popularity in this country is bound to be accompanied by movement, since it makes you want to move. This dance is an original one created to this music by Winifred Hooper, of Jamaica, while she was a student at New York University. The dance is adaptable to other calypso records, since it is free of specific interpretation of words. The constant motions of the hips, which flow from side to side, and the rib cage, which moves in opposition to the hips, are characteristic of calypso dancing. The basic step that is used is explained on page 29. Combined with this is a simple walk forward or backward with opposition hip shift. Most often it is a combination of single steps and two-steps with hips and weight following the step. You are free to take this liberty spontaneously.

Partners face each other in a double circle, men on the inside. Join hands and stretch arms sideward.

Fig. 1. At the beginning of the music, dance four basic steps (see page 52) away from partner and four toward partner. Arms stretch fwd when you move bkwd, sdwd when you move fwd.

Free dance: Dance in closed position, with partner turning in place with basic step, and let yourself go with the full swing of the music. This is done to one full phrase of the music.

FIG. 2. Holding elbows straight, with hands joined, dance four basic steps fwd toward partner as arms move out to sides. Touch foreheads together on the fourth step and dance four basic steps bkwd; then turn with partner four times in place in same hand position.

Repeat free dance until you want to change.

FIG. 3. Women place hands on hips, sway the hips gracefully while dancing in place; men raise hands overhead and dance freely (improvise) before their partners.

Repeat free dance.

FIG. 4. Man holds woman at waist, and woman places hands on man's shoulders. Rock from left to right four times and circle in waist position.

Repeat from beginning.

Note: This is an informal dance. Much communication takes place through subtle gesture, depending on the creativity and uninhibited character of the dancers. You are free to interpret music as you feel it. The theme is the rhythmical movement of the hips. To do this, you must relax. Also, phrasing is not clear cut: you can add a step or continue repeating pretty much as you feel it.

PARISIAN POLKA [1] (Denmark)

Records: Folk Dancer MH-1046
Kismet 140

Couples are back to back in a circle with inside hands joined forward. Direction of travel is CC; free hand is on hip. Man starts left and the woman starts right. The man's part is described; the woman does the counterpart except when specifically noted.

FIG. 1. Seven polka steps alternately face to face and back to back; jump toward partner, and jump away from partner.

Repeat figure, ending on jumps, with man facing CC and woman facing CW.

---

[1] Fred Leifer, *The Folk Dance Memorizer* (Brooklyn, N. Y.: Brooklyn College, 1951), p. 34.

FIG. 2. Man and woman do polka step to own right, step fwd R, step bkwd L; polka to own L, step fwd L, bkwd R.

FIG. 3. Cross hands—man's R with woman's R.
Do eight polka steps CC, man going fwd starting L and woman going bkwd starting R. On each polka, change the hand grasp from R with R to L with L, re-grasping on each step.

FIG. 4. Polka step L, point L heel fwd, L toe across R foot.
Polka step R, point R heel fwd, and R toe across L foot.

Repeat.

Eight polka steps turning CW, traveling in a CC direction.

GREEN SLEEVES [2] (English-American Country Dance)
Record: Methodist M 106
Victor 45-6175

This dance is to be done with a quality similar to that of Contra dancing. It is comfortable in tempo and may be done very gracefully. It is characteristic of English dancing in its use of a smooth walking step.

Couples are in a double circle, facing CC. Two couples make a set. Couples must know to which set they belong. Couple 1 is in front of couple 2. Woman is on the right of the man. Join inside hands and hold them at shoulder height. Start with the outside foot (left for man, right for woman).

FIG. 1. Walk 16 steps fwd.

FIG. 2. Star with the R hand; in each set of two couples, the couple in front turns bkwd and they place their R hands in the center, forming a pivot point (see page 66 for star) with the couple in back. Walk CW 8 steps. Change to L hand in center and walk CC 8 steps.

FIG. 3. Turn sleeves: couple 1, with hands joined, bends down and walks four steps bkwd under the arch made by couple 2. Couple 1 arches and walks fwd four steps while couple 2 goes under arch bkwd. Couples are now back to place. Repeat this figure once.

Repeat dance continuously to end of music.

---

[2] Fred Leifer, *The Folk Dance Memorizer* (Brooklyn, N. Y.: Brooklyn College, 1951), p. 15.

BOSTON TWO-STEP [3] (England)

Records: Columbia DX1191
Folk Dancer MH 3001
MacGregor 309

This dance should be done smoothly, gracefully, and with the politeness and elegance of the old-time quadrilles.

Couples are in a circle facing CC with inside hands joined at shoulder level.

Start on the outside foot (man's left, woman's right). Man's part is described. Woman does counterpart except where specifically noted.

> PAS-DE-BAS STEP: Take a small leap sdwd L (1).
> Cross R foot in front of L, taking weight for a very short time on the ball of the R foot (&).
> Step in place L (2).

> FIG. 1. One Pas-De-Bas away from partner and one toward partner (man L, woman R).
> With outside foot, take three steps fwd, pivoting on the third toward partner to face CW. Point the outside foot fwd.

> Repeat from beginning, starting with the other foot (man R, woman L).

> FIG. 2. Face partner with hands joined: Pas-De-Pas to man's L and repeat to R. Step L sdwd, Cl R to L, step L sdwd, Cl R to L.
> In closed position, do four two-steps, turning CW and traveling CC.

EVA THREE STEP (English-Canadian)

Record: Columbia DX 1257

This is an old-time dance that has all the elegance and propriety of the English dances in the music. The music helps you feel the mood of the dance. This dance is presented as it was taught by Howard Smith of Potsdam, New York.

Couples are in a circle facing CC.

Woman is on the right of the man. Inside hands are joined and raised to shoulder height. Begin on the outside foot (L for man, R for woman). Man's part is described. Woman does counterpart, except when specifically noted.

> FIG. 1. Walk fwd four steps starting L.
> Man: Walk diagonally fwd R four steps, crossing in back of partner.
> Woman: Walk diagonally fwd L four steps.

---

[3] Fred Leifer, *The Folk Dance Memorizer* (Brooklyn, N. Y.: Brooklyn College, 1951), p. 7.

Man: Walk diagonally fwd L four steps, crossing in back of partner.

Woman: Walk diagonally fwd R four steps.

Walk fwd three steps, turn to face partner.

FIG. 2. BALANCE AND TWO-STEP:
Step L, swing R foot across L.
Step R, swing L foot across R.

Repeat figure.

Take four two-steps, turning CW and traveling CC.

ALFELDER [4] (Germany)   Record: Methodist 115

Alfelder is a traditional folk game from the town of Alfeld, near Hanover, Germany.

Dancers are in groups of three (man in middle and woman on each side) standing side by side in a large circle. One group of three faces another as a set of six within a circle.

FIG. 1. CIRCLE: Each group of six join hands and circle CW eight steps and CC eight steps, ending in two lines again.

FIG. 2. ELBOW TURN: Two men hook R elbows and turn CW with four steps; hook L elbows with woman on R and turn CC with four steps; hook R elbows with woman on their L and turn CC with four steps; go back in line in four steps.

FIG. 3. PASS THROUGH: Bow to opposite trio (four counts) and pass through, passing R shoulders with person opposite in eight steps; new trio will be met; bow (four counts).

BUMMEL SCHOTTISCHE [5] (Germany)   Record: Victor 45-6177

Couples are in a large circle with the woman in front of the man. He places his hands on her waist and she places her hands on his. Both start on same foot.

FIG. 1. Place L heel fwd (woman looks over shoulder at partner), tap floor with L toe.
Take one Schottische L sdwd.

---

[4] Audio-Visual Department, Division of Local Church General Board of Education, The Methodist Church, World of Fun (Nashville, Tennessee: the Methodist Publishing House, 1951), p. 34.

[5] RCA, Dance Descriptions (Camden, N.J.: Radio Corporation of America, 1952), form number 3s-759H.

Repeat figure, starting R and looking over R shoulder.
Repeat from beginning.

FIG. 2. Do eight polka steps around the room. You may keep the position
of Figure 1 or change to shoulder-waist position, facing partner
on the end of the phrase of Figure 1.

SIEBENSHRITT [6] (Germany)   *Records:* Methodist 101
                                                   Folk Dancer MH 1048

Siebenshritt is commonly known as *Seven Steps* and is based entirely on a running step. This step should be done lightly and close to the floor.

Couples are in a circle, standing side by side and facing CC. The woman is on the right of the man, and inside hands are joined. Begin on outside foot (left for man, right for woman).

FIG. 1. Seven running steps fwd and hold count 8. Seven running steps
bkwd and hold count 8.

FIG. 2. Drop hands and separate from partner (woman diagonally fwd
R to outside and man diagonally fwd L to inside of circle) with a
Schottische step.

Repeat the schottische, coming toward partner.
Take shoulder-waist position and do four step-hops in a circle CW.

Repeat the Schottische away from partner.
When coming back, woman does Schottische toward man in
front of her and the man goes to woman behind him. Do four
step-hops with new partner.

Repeat from beginning.

KRITIKOS [7] (Greek)   *Records:* Folkraft 1021
                                                   Columbia 10072
                                                   Kismet 142

Kritikos is also known as *Miserlou,* which is the name of the music used to accompany the dance. This dance is typical of Greek circle dances, which are scarcely seen in this country. If Greek dances exist at all, they exist temporarily

---

[6] Fred Leifer, *The Folk Dance Memorizer* (Brooklyn, N. Y.: Brooklyn College, 1951), p. 37.
[7] Jane A. Harris, Ann Pittman, and Marlys S. Waller, *Dance A While.* Minnesota: Burgess Publishing Company, 1950, p. 159.

at festivities of the Greek groups in this country. The music for their dances has a plaintive quality. The dances rely on the varying length of syllables for inflection and rhythmic sentence; if the syllable is stressed, the step is stressed.[8] Kritikos consists of one phrase of movement repeated over and over. Only the direction is varied. It is a quiet, smooth dance.

Dancers are in a single circle with one break in the circle. All others join hands and face center. The circle moves CC with a person at the head as leader. He leads the line of dancers CC into a spiral, making the circle smaller and smaller, and then leads them CW into a larger circle again. He is free to determine where the line will go. The counts are included because they are difficult to find in the music. Everyone does the same step pattern and begins on the same foot.

Step in place R (1-2).
Point L toe in front of R and circle L foot around CC on the floor (3-4).
Step L behind R (1), step R in place (2), step L across in front of R (3).
Turn body ¼ CC (4).
Step fwd R, Cl L to R, step fwd R (1,2,3, hold 4).
Step bkwd L, Cl R to L, step fdwd L (1,2,3, hold 4).

CSEBOGAR [9] (Hungary)   *Records:* Methodist 101
                                                      Folkraft 196
                                                      Victor 45-6182

Partners are in a single circle facing center; the woman is on the right of the man. Hands are joined in the circle.

FIG. 1. Eight slides to the L (CW).
         Eight slides to the R (CC).
         Four skips toward center.
         Four skips bkwd to place.
         Hungarian turn: Partners face each other and place R arm around partner's waist with R sides together. Raise L arm upward. Take one hop R, step L, step R (hop-step-step). Repeat three times.

FIG. 2. Partners take shoulder-waist position (see page 81).
         Man's L shoulder is toward center, as is woman's R shoulder.

---

[8] Joan Lawson, *European Folk Dances.* London: Pitman Press, 1953, p. 67.
[9] Adapted from Dorothy LaSalle, *Rhythms and Dances for Elementary Schools,* Second Edition. Copyright 1951, The Ronald Press Company, p. 118.

Step toward center with L, close R to L (step, close).
Repeat step-close three times.
Repeat step-close, moving away from center, four times starting R.
Repeat step-close toward center twice and away from center twice.
Do Hungarian turn four times and finish with shout.

CZARDAS [10] (Hungary)

Records: Kismet 107
Folkraft 1196

Couples any place on the floor. Take skater's position (see page 79). Man and woman begin with same foot.

FIG. 1. Step fwd L, Cl R to L, and repeat step-close. Take 3 hops in place on L foot while you cross R foot in front of L, point R sdwd, and bring R to L, clicking heels (Bokazni step).

Repeat this figure three times, starting L.

FIG. 2. Face partner and place hands on own hips. Take four steps bkwd and a Bokazni step R.
Turn in place CW with four steps and a Bokazni R.
Take two steps toward partner and three stamps in place (R,L,R,L,R) and one Bokazni R.

Four dipping turns: Partners face each other, place hand around each other's waist with R sides together and L arm raised overhead. Step down R bending the knee and step high on the ball of L foot. Alternate the down-up dip, taking eight steps in all, turning in place.

Repeat Figure 2.

IRISH LONG DANCE [11] (Ireland)

Record: Victor 17840
Imperial 1040

This is a joyous dance and typical of the longways country dance. Partners are facing each other in sets of two couples.

FIG. 1. Hop L as you tap R toe in front of L.
Hop L as you swing R around in back of L, taking weight.
In this crossed position, take four steps in place, L,R,L,R.

---

[10] Fred Leifer, *The Folk Dance Memorizer* (Brooklyn, N. Y.: Brooklyn College, 1951), p. 10.
[11] Adapted from Anne S. Duggan, Jeannette Schlottmann, and Abbie Rutledge, *Folk Dances of the British Isles*. New York: The Ronald Press, 1948, p. 95.

Repeat the above, starting with hop R.

Form R-hand star and do four polkas CW.

FIG. 2. Couple 1 joins hands, takes four slides down the set between couple 2, and four slides back again.
Couple 1 slides down again, while couple 2 slides up the outside of the set.
Couple 1 slides up the outside as couple 2 slides down the inside of the set.

FIG. 3. Take shoulder-waist position with partner.
Do eight polkas in small circle, turning CW and traveling CC
Finish in the other couple's position.

Repeat dance, ending in your own place.

SICILIAN TARANTELLA [12] (Italy)   Record: Victor V-12567

This is a simple version of the tarantella. It is gay and flirtatious and leaves room for improvisation. Finger snapping may be substituted for use of tambourines.

Sets of two couples, with men on one side and women on the other. Everyone begins with L foot. Face partner.

FIG. 1. Step in place with L foot as you clap hands (women, tambourines); hop L as you swing R foot across L.

Repeat above step, starting R.

Four running steps in place, L,R,L,R (men snap fingers, women tambourines).

Repeat from beginning three times.

FIG. 2. Take four running steps toward partner, bending fwd at knees and hips; snap fingers and/or shake tambourines while running.
Take four running steps bkwd as body straightens.
Again use finger snapping and/or tambourines.

Repeat figure three times.

FIG. 3. Man of couple 1 and woman of couple 2 take eight running steps to complete the following: run to center, hook right elbows, turn once around CW, and return to position.

---

[12] Michael Herman, *Folk Dances for All* (New York: Barnes and Noble, Inc., 1947), p. 48.

Repeat with man of couple 2 and woman of couple 1.

Repeat whole figure, hooking left elbows.

FIG. 4. Man of couple 1 and woman of couple 2 dos-a-dos * (see page 62).
Man of couple 2 and woman of couple 1 dos-a-dos.

Repeat figure but pass left shoulders (or reverse of dos-a-dos).

FIG. 5. Take eight skipping steps CC with L shoulder to center and hands on own hips.
Reverse with R shoulder to center, skip eight steps back to place.

FIG. 6. Form a left-hand star (see page 66) and skip eight steps CC (women shaking tambourines). Form a right-hand star and skip eight times CW.

POTCH TANZ [13] (Israel) Record: Folkraft 5001A-A

This Potch Tanz (clap dance) is a circle dance in couples created to an Israeli melody by Dvora Lapson. The Potch Tanz is a lively dance with clapping and stamping and is popular at Jewish weddings in Eastern Europe.

Couples are in a single circle with the woman on the right of the man. Everyone faces the center of the circle.

FIGURE 1

Ladies take four steps to center, starting R,
Clap hands and stamp feet three times (simultaneously).
Ladies take four steps bkwd to place; clap and stamp three times.

Men repeat all of the above.

Partners take skaters' position, with left elbow bent and right elbow straight; take 16 running steps, moving the circle to the left.
Reverse, with right elbow bent and left elbow straight; take 16 running steps circling R.

FIGURE 2

Everyone take four steps to center; clap and stamp three times.
Form a star with the right hand up in center and take eight steps CW.
Reverse, making a left-hand star and walking eight steps CC.
Everyone take four steps backward; clap hands and stamp three times.

---

[13] Dvora Lapson, *Dances of the Jewish People.* New York: The Jewish Education Committee, 1954, pp. 39-40.

Partners face each other, place R hands on R shoulders, and circle in place with 16 running steps CW.

Reverse, place left hand on partner's shoulder, and run 16 steps CC.

FIGURE 3

Everyone take four steps into center; clap hands and stamp three times.
Everyone take four steps bkwd; clap and stamp three times.

Repeat from beginning of figure.

* Join hands in circle at shoulder level; balance R (step R, close L, step in place R), balance L (step L, close R, step in place L), turn slightly R, and take four running steps CC.

Repeat from *, running CW.

SHIBOLET BASADEH [14] (Israel)   *Record:* Folkraft 1109B

"This dance is performed during the Omer Ceremony in Israel and is a revival of an ancient festival on Passover, when the first sheaves of barley were cut in the fields and presented to the Holy Temple." [15]

Single circle, no partners needed. Join hands, letting them hang down.

A. Moving CC, take three side-close steps and step-hop turn; step R sdwd, Cl L to R.
   Repeat twice. Drop hands and step and hop on R while turning ½ CW. The circle is now facing outward.

   Repeat the whole sequence, starting L and moving CC.

   Repeat from the beginning.

B. Move CC with step-hop and hands joined.
   Face slightly R, take two step-hops fwd in line of direction, starting R. On second hop, turn ½ left. Take two step-hops bkwd in line of direction (CC) and turn ½ R on second hop.

   Repeat the four step-hops.

[14] Dvora Lapson, *Dances of the Jewish People.* New York: The Jewish Education Committee, 1954, pp. 15-16.
[15] *Ibid.,* p. 15.

C. Facing center of circle, go in and out. Take two step-hops toward center, raising joined hands.

Take four step-hops bkwd, away from center. Dance is repeated over and over as tempo increases gradually.

MI PECOSITA [16] (Mexican)   *Record:* ASP 102

This is a typical polka danced in northern Mexico. It is most fluently seen in the states of Chihuahua, Sonora, and Durango.

Couples are in a circle in closed position. Man faces CC, woman CW. Directions are given for the man. Woman does the counterpart except where specifically noted.

FIG. 1. MEXICAN POLKA: This is actually a two-step but with short steps and bouncing movement from the knees.

Starting L, take eight Mexican Polka steps CC, letting the body sway in the direction of each step.

Take eight more polkas, turning CW but traveling CC.

Repeat figure, ending with man's back to center.

FIG. 2. Heel-toe slide—closed position.

Extend L heel sideward as you hop on R,

Extend L toe sideward as you hop on R.

Repeat both.

Four slides to man's L.

Repeat figure from beginning, starting R.

Repeat whole figure three times, ending with man facing CC and woman CW.

FIG. 3. Turn—closed position.

Four Mexican polkas CC.

Man: Four Mexican polkas in place.

Woman: Four Mexican polkas, turning. Man's L and woman's R hands joined.

Both take four Mexican polkas in closed position, turning CW and traveling CC.

Repeat the four Mexican polkas in place, with woman turning under arm.

[16] The Folk Dance Federation of California, *Let's Dance Magazine*, February 1958.

J. M. HODGES LIBRARY
WHARTON COUNTY JUNIOR COLLEGE
WHARTON, TEXAS

Repeat the whole figure, ending with man and woman standing side by side facing CC. Man's and woman's L hands joined and raised fwd. Right hands joined at woman's R side.

FIG. 4. Touch-hop-slide: Man and woman start with L foot.
Point L foot fwd, hop on R as L knee is raised.

Repeat.

Take four slide steps diagonally fwd L, with man cutting in back of woman to end on her R. Right arms are now fwd and L at waist.

Repeat figure, starting R.

Repeat whole figure 3 times.

FIG. 5. Around each other.
Partners face, in separated position. Man's hands clasped behind back; woman holds skirt. Both do same steps on same foot. With the following step, they go around each other CW.

Leap diagonally fwd L, Cl R to L, step L in place.
Leap diagonally fwd R, Cl L to R, step R in place.

Repeat from beginning, ending with man facing CC and woman opposite.
Two Mexican polkas—one toward partner, one away from partner.
Repeat two polkas.

Repeat whole figure three times, ending with man's back to center in closed position.

FIG. 6. Heel-toe, glide, and polka.
Hop R, extending L heel sdwd, hop R extending L toe sdwd bending L knee and
Hop R, extending L heel sdwd, chug R sdwd, bringing L foot to R shin.
Take four slides to L.

Repeat, starting R.

Repeat from beginning of figure.

Take four Mexican polka steps CC in CL position.

Take four Mexican polka steps, traveling CC, turning CW.
Take four Mexican polka steps CC.
Man: Take three Mexican polka steps in place and bow.
Woman: Take three Mexican polka steps, turning CW under
man's L arm, and curtsy.

KOHANOCHKA [17] (Russian)

Records: MH 1058
Kismet 101

Kohanochka is a Russian ballroom dance. There is a distinction between the ballroom and the peasant dances of Russia: ballroom dances are smooth, graceful, and simple. Kohanochka ("beloved") is representative of this type. It should be danced with constant flowing movement.

Couples are arranged in a large circle side by side, facing CC, inside hands joined. Begin on outside foot. The man's part is described. Woman does the counterpart except when specifically noted.

FIG. 1. Step fwd L, Cl R to L, step fwd L (step-close-step), while swinging inside arms fwd (at shoulder level).
Repeat, starting R and swinging joined hands bkwd (at shoulder level).
Swing inside hands fwd and release as you make full turn away from partner in two two-steps.

Repeat figure.

FIG. 2. Shoulder position:
Step fwd L raising R foot in back.
Step bkwd R raising L foot in front.
Step-close-step L.
Step-close-step R.

Repeat figure.

FIG. 3. Partners face each other, man with back to center.
Clap your hands twice.
Take three two-steps bkwd away from partner. (Woman holds skirt; man crosses arms on chest.)
Clap hands twice.
Take three two-steps fwd, passing partner by L shoulder.
Clap hands twice.

---

[17] Michael Herman, *Folk Dances for All*. New York: Barnes and Noble, Inc., 1947, pp. 63-65.

Take three two-steps bkwd, passing partner by L shoulder.
Clap hands twice.
Pause.
Take two two-steps (CC) making a full turn away from partner,
    as in Fig. 1.

GIE GORDONS (Scotland)   *Record:* Beltona 2455

This dance, similar in character to The Roberts, is more difficult to do well but just as enjoyable to watch as to dance. This dance is written as it was danced by two members of Howard Smith's Potsdam Polka Dots at the International Folk Festival in 1951 at Canton, New York.

Take shoulder position.* Begin on outside foot (man left, woman right). Man's part is described. Woman's part is opposite unless specifically noted.

FIG. 1. PRANCE WITH PIVOT:
    Step fwd L, raising R knee high with toes pointing downward;
        step R, raising L knee high.
    Repeat L and R. On the last step R, pivot CW one-half turn (both
        man and woman). The woman is on the L of the man.
    Take four prance steps bkwd.

    Repeat whole figure.

FIG. 2. TURNING:
    Man: Drops woman's L hand and places his L on own hip; takes
        eight prance steps, moving slightly fwd on each step and
        shaking head ** sdwd four times to each step.

    Woman: Takes four full turns CW while doing eight prance steps.
    Both swing into closed position and do three two-steps, turning
        CW. Man pivots partner under R arm into shoulder position
        again.

    Repeat dance. With each repetition of the dance, the tempo of
        the music is gradually increased.

THE ROBERTS (Scotland)   *Records:* Beltona 2457
                                      Windsor R 607

This dance is also known as *Rik-Ma-Ree,* which is actually the name of the music. It has a specific Scotch flavor, provided that the movement is done with

---

* See page 80.
** See Roberts, page 107.

the quality of a Highland Fling. The dance is presented here as it is done in northern New York and Canada and as it was taught by Howard Smith, director of the Potsdam Polka Dots, in 1951. The first record listed above uses piano, accordion, and drums and comes as close as possible to sounding like bagpipes. Start on the outside foot.

FIG. 1. PRANCE:
Step L fwd (1).
Close R to L, lifting L knee high with toes pointing to ground (2).

Repeat (3-4).

Four prances (high steps lifting knees as above), circling away from partner, L,R,L,R (1-4).
Hands are on hips, head shakes from side to side (four times to each step).

Repeat whole figure.

FIG. 2. HEEL-TOE AND TWO-STEP.
Place L heel diagonally fwd L (1).
Cross L toe over R (2).
Two-step fwd L (3 and 4).

Repeat, starting R (1-4).

Four two-steps circling CW, starting L.

Repeat from beginning. The music gradually becomes faster.

Note: The sideward head shake means that the left ear is dropped toward the left shoulder and then the right ear toward the right shoulder. The movement is small and quick.

ERSKO KOLO [18] (Yugoslavia)   *Record:* Folk Dancer MH 3020

Single circle; no partners needed. All join hands, facing center. Hands are held straight down to sides; dancers stand as tall as possible. This dance is arrogant in feeling.

FIG. 1. The circle gradually moves CC with 14 steps and two stamps. The steps are done as follows:
Take a small step sdwd reaching for the floor with heel of R

---

[18] Michael Herman, *Folk Dance Series.* New York: The Folk Dance House, 1957.

foot; bring L foot to R. Follow the 14 steps with a stamp R and L in place.

Repeat figure CW.

FIG. 2. Hands are still joined; facing slightly to the R, take one Schottische step fwd and one bkwd.
Face center of circle and take one Schottische into center and one bkwd away from center.

Repeat from beginning.

Note: "A handkerchief plays an important part in many Yugoslav Kolos. It is carried by the leader, is carefully twisted and waved to the rhythm of the dance, and is passed on to the next dancer should the leader decide his powers are failing." [19]

SELECTED RECORDS FOR FOLK DANCE

The following selected records are suggested for further folk dancing. In practically all cases, the directions come with the purchase of records.

Folkraft 1108 *Mayim* (Israel), *Levshee Na'os* (Debka), *Hanodeid* (line dance)
Folk Dancer MH-1058 ⎱ *Kohanochka*
Kismet 101   ⎰ (Russian)
Folk Dancer MH-1059 *Korobushka* (Russian - American), *Troika*
MH-3003 *Road to the Isles* (Scotch), *Rocking Waltz*
MH-2001 *Telemark Schottische* (Norway), *Norwegian Polka*
MH-1021 *Totur* (Danish), *Sextur*
Imperial 1137 *Corrido* (Mexican), (Same as *Eso-Si-Eso-No*)

Methodist—LP-12" *World of Fun Series* (with instruction booklet)
M-101 *Cshebogar, Kalvelis, Hol-di-ri-dia* (seven steps)
M-107 *Little Brown Jug, Put Your Little Foot, The Fireman's Dance*
M-108 *Seven Jumps, Korobushka, Gustav's Skol, Crested Hen*
M-110 *Hopak, Newcastle, Road to the Isles, Spinning Waltz*
M-115 *Alfelder, At the Inn "To the Crown," Sonderburg Double Quadrille*
RCA Victor Michael Herman, Folk Dance Orchestra, *World of Folk Dances* (all with instructions).

---

[19] Joan Lawson, *European Folk Dance*. London: Pitman Press, 1953, p. 77.

RCA Victor LPM-1619 *Special Folk Dances*
12 Dances from Philippines, Germany, Italy, Poland, Hungary, Sweden, Mexico, Scotland, Estonia.
EPA-4126 *Special Folk Dances*
12 Dances from Greece, Ser-

bia, Portugal, Scotland, America, Ireland, Holland.
RCA Victor EPA-4127 *Advanced Folk Dances:* Bavarian Ländler (Germany), Krakowiak (Poland), Tivoli Hambo (Sweden), El Jarabe Tapatio (Mexico).

SELECTED SOURCES FOR FOLK DANCES

Alford, Violet (ed.), *Handbooks of European National Dances.* New York: Chanticleer Press, 1948-1952.
Dances of Austria, by Katharina Breuer.
Dances of Bulgaria, by Raina Katsarvoua.
Dances of Czechoslovakia, by Mila Lubinova.
Dances of Denmark, by Lorenzen and Jeppe Jeppesen.
Dances of England and Wales, by Maud Karpeles and Lois Blake.
Dances of Finland, by Yngvar Heikel.
Dances of France I: Brittany and Bourbonnais, by Claudie Marcel DuBois and Marguerite Andral.
Dances of France II: Provence and Alsace, by Nicolette Tennevin and Marie Texier.
Dances of Germany, by Agnes Fyte.
Dances of Greece, by Domini Crosfield.
Dances of Hungary, by George Buday.
Dances of Italy, by Bianca M. Galanti.
Dances of Netherlands, by E. Vander Ven-ten Bensel.
Dances of Portugal, by Lucille Armstrong.
Dances of Spain I: South, Centre and Northwest, by Lucille Armstrong.
Dances of Spain II: North-east and East, by Lucille Armstrong.
Dances of Sweden, by Erik Salven.
Dances of Switzerland, by Louise Witzig.
——————, *Pyreneen Festivals: Calendar*

Customs, Music and Magic, Drama and Dance. London: Chatto and Windus, 1937.
Allan's Collection: Reels and Strathspeys, Quadrilles, Waltzes, Country Dances, Highland Schottisches, Jigs, Hornpipes. With accordion markings. Glasgow: Mozart Allan.
Armstrong, Lucille, *Dances of Portugal.* New York: Chanticleer Press, 1948.
——————, *Dances of Spain.* New York: Chanticleer Press, 1950.
Burchenal, Elizabeth, *Folk Dances of Germany.* New York: G. Schirmer, Inc., 1938.
——————, *National Dances of Ireland.* New York: G. Schirmer, Inc., 1929.
—————— (ed.), *Twenty-eight Contra-Dances, largely from New England States.* New York: G. Schirmer, Inc., 1945.
Burchenal, Elizabeth, *Folk Dances from Old Homelands.* New York: G. Schirmer, Inc., 1922.
Chalif, Louis Harvey, *Russian Festivals and Costumes for Pageant and Dance.* New York: Chalif Russian School of Dancing, 1921.
Chochem, Corinne, *Jewish Holiday Dances.* New York: Behrman House, Inc., 1948.
——————, *Palestine Dances!* New York: Behrman's Jewish Book House, 1941.
Czarnowski, Lucille K., *Dances of Early*

California Days. Palo Alto, California: Pacific Books, 1950.

Delakova, Katya, and Fred Berk, *Dances of Palestine*. New York: B'nai B'rith Hillel Foundations, 1947.

Duggan, Anne S., Jeanette Schlottmann, and Abbie Rutledge, *Folk Dances of the British Isles*. New York: Ronald Press, 1948.

————, *Folk Dances of European Countries*. New York: Ronald Press, 1948.

————, *Folk Dances of Scandinavia*. New York: Ronald Press, 1948.

————, *Folk Dances of United States and Mexico*. New York: Ronald Press, 1948.

————, *The Teaching of Folk Dance*. New York: Ronald Press, 1948.

Dunsing, Paul, *German Folk Dances*. Leipzig: F. Hofmeister, 1936.

———— and Gretel, *Dance Lightly*. Delaware, Ohio: Cooperative Recreation Service, 1946 (handbook).

Durlacher, Ed, *Honor Your Partner*. New York: Devin-Adair, 1949.

Fox, Grace I., *Folk Dancing*, 2nd ed. New York: Ronald Press, 1957.

Glinski, Tomasz, *Polish Folk Dances*. London: Maxwell, Love and Co., 1946. Music and words (Polish and English).

Harris, Jane A., Anne Pittman, and Marlys S. Waller, *Dance A While*, 2nd ed. Minneapolis: Burgess Publishing Co., 1950.

Herman, Michael, *Folk Dances for All*. New York: Barnes and Noble, Inc., 1947.

————, ed., *Folk Dance Syllabus No. 1*. New York: The Folk Dance House, 1953. (70 Folk Dances, 15 Contras, 7 Squares)

Lager, Herbert, *Our Austrian Dances*. Millbrae, California: National Press, 1952.

Lapson, Dvora, *Dances of the Jewish People*. New York: Jewish Education Committee, 1954.

LaSalle, Dorothy, *Rhythms and Dances for Elementary Schools*. 2nd ed. New York: Ronald Press, 1951.

Lawson, Joan, *European Folk Dance; its National and Musical Characteristics*. London: Pitman, 1953.

Leifer, Fred, *The Folk Dance Memorizer*. Brooklyn, N. Y.: Brooklyn College, 1951.

MacKenzie, Donald R., *Highland Dances*. Glasgow: A. MacLaren, 1939.

Maclachlan, Elizabeth, *The Border Dance Book; Scottish Country Dances*. Edinburgh: McDougall's Co., 1935.

Mac Lennan, D. G., *Dances of Scotland*. London: M. Parrish & Co., 1950.

Milligan, Jean C., *Dances of Scotland*. London: M. Parrish & Co., 1950.

O'Rafferty, Peadar, *Dances of Ireland*. London: M. Parrish & Co., 1953.

Pinon, Roger, *Dances of Belgium*. London: M. Parrish & Co., 1953.

Reyes, Aquino Francisca, *Fundamental Dance Steps*. Manila, The Philippines: 1954.

————, *Philippine Folk Dances*. Manila: 1950.

Sedillo, Mela C., *Mexican and New Mexican Folk Dances*. Albuquerque, New Mexico: University of New Mexico Press, 1950.

Semb, Klara, *Dances of Norway*. London: M. Parrish & Co., 1951.

Tolentino, Francisca, *Philippine National Dances*. New York: Silver Burdett Co., 1946.

Vizonsky, Nathan, *Ten Jewish Folk Dances*. Chicago: American-Hebrew Theatrical League, 1942.

Wolska, Helen, *Dances of Poland*. London: M. Parrish & Co., 1952.

CHAPTER VIII

Tap Dance

Tap dancing, although you know it from vaudeville and television as a form of entertainment, actually descended from folk steps of various countries—primarily through the jig, clog, and shuffle steps. It is probably most closely related to the Irish jig, in which the sound made by the feet is of great importance in the style and character of the dance. Although the terminology of tap dance and that of jig dancing are similar, the former uses popular music and the latter uses folk music, giving a completely different character to the two dances.

Rhythm is necessarily a part of every type of dancing, but in tap dancing it is of primary importance. If you are not accurate rhythmically, tap dancing is no fun at all. For that reason it is abso-lutely necessary to conquer basic steps so that you feel the rhythm and can do the step to music. If you want to tap well, be sure to learn the basic steps thoroughly. When you know them, you can enjoy many hours creating your own dances—which is far more satisfying and rewarding than interpreting a dance from the written page. It pays to take several basic steps as you learn them and put them into simple combinations.

When moving rhythmically, it is necessary to keep a constant pulse or beat somewhere in the body. This can be a verbal count, a click of the tongue, a grunt, or whatever you have a tendency to do. Remember that this beat is your rhythmic measure as you learn basic steps. To be effective, you must keep this beat as steady as a metronome that clicks off at regular intervals. You will have a tendency to count slower when you are having trouble co-ordinating or remembering and faster when you are sure of yourself. Get used to counting or marking rhythm aloud at a steady tempo. Practice this before you begin to practice steps.

The following description of steps is organized according to the number of sounds made by the feet in executing these steps. Each step, taken singly, is not in the least difficult until you get to buck and triple-time steps. The difficulty that you will encounter is doing a sequence of steps without breaking the rhythm.

The basic steps in tap dancing call for a type of co-ordination different from what the average person is used to doing. The ankle must be flexible, since most of the foot action is one of raising and lowering the foot while you swing the lower leg forward, backward, or sideward. Remember to keep the action of the legs small and to work with the ankles. Many people make the error of trying to tap dance by swinging the leg from the hip. The action of the tap rhythm is in the ankles and feet primarily. Practice standing on one foot and lifting the toe of the free foot up and down to get used to this type of action.

BASIC STEPS—ONE SOUND

BRUSH

With weight on one foot, brush the ball of the free foot against the floor. Practice in all directions to get an even brush. A brush may be forward, sideward, or backward.

CHUG

With the weight on one foot, bend the knee and push the heel into the floor as you scoot a few inches diagonally forward. A chug can also be sideward. Practice on each leg. Do several chug steps consecutively.

HEEL

With the weight on the balls of the feet and heels raised, dig heels into floor. This may also be done singly or alternately.

HOP

With the weight on one foot, push off the floor with that foot and land on the same foot.

JUMP

With the weight on both feet, push off the floor and land on both feet. This may also be done by pushing off one foot, but in any case the landing must be on two feet at the same time.

LEAP

With the weight on one foot, push off the floor and land on the other foot.

PULL

With the weight on one foot with knee bent, the free foot is off the floor and reaching backward. Pull the body backward diagonally by raising the free leg and taking a little lift in the body. The standing foot slides along the floor. This is the opposite of a chug step. Here you pull instead of push.

STEP

With the weight on one foot, shift the weight onto the other foot. This transfer of weight may also be taken by stamping.

TAP

With the weight on one foot, drop the toe of the free foot to the floor. Do a series of toe taps.

BASIC STEPS—TWO SOUNDS

BALL-CHANGE

With the weight on one foot, place the ball of the free foot on the floor, taking the weight on that foot momentarily; shift the weight back to the other foot again. The rhythm is *short-long*, that is, the weight is taken on the ball of the foot for a very short time and the change to the other foot is longer (count is *and 1*).

BANDY TURN

With the weight on the left foot, do the ball-change step four times, turning clockwise on each change by rotating the right leg outward on each step. (This is commonly known as a *buzz-step* in square dancing.)

BELL

With the weight left, step across and in front of left with right foot, lift the left leg sideward as you push off the floor with the right foot, clicking heels in the air (by bringing right to left), and landing on the right foot again. This is actually a step-click-hop (count *1 and 2*) and can be done in 2/4 or 3/4 time.

   or

BRUSH-BACK

With the weight on one foot, brush the free foot backward; then take a step backward.

DOUBLE

With the weight on one foot, brush the ball of the free foot forward and backward.

SPANK

With the weight on one foot, brush the ball of the free foot forward and immediately take the weight on the ball of that foot. Do a series of spanks forward, alternating right and left, at running tempo (count is *and 1*).

TOE-HEEL

With the weight on the left foot, take a toe tap with the right foot followed by a heel step, shifting the weight to the right foot.

BASIC STEPS—THREE OR MORE SOUNDS

BUFFALO

With the weight on the right foot, leap sideward onto the left foot (count *1*); do a double with the right foot (*and, a*); and leap onto the right, which passes in back of left (*2*); as you leap to the right foot, the left knee bends and the left foot is brought up and across in front of the left. There are four sounds to this step (count is *1 and a two*). The step pattern is *leap, double, leap*.

GRAPEVINE

Step left sideward on the heel of the left foot, cross the right foot in back of left; step sideward left again, cross right in front of left; step sideward left again and cross right in back of left. This may be done in a variety of rhythmic patterns.

SHUFFLE

With the weight on the left foot, take a double right, hop left, step in place right. Repeat, starting left. The step pattern is double-hop-step (count *1 and a 2*).

THREE-STEP TURN

With the weight left, step right sideward, turning the leg outward; bring the left leg around clockwise and toe inward toward the right (½ turn is completed); pivot clockwise on the left and step sideward right with the right foot. Steps are even; repeat to the other side.

WALTZ TIME STEP

With the weight right, take a small leap in place on the left foot followed by a double and ball change on the right foot. The step pattern is *leap-double-ball change* (count *1 and 2 and 3*). Repeat on alternate sides.

BUCK SINGLE TIME STEP

With the weight right, take a double forward with the left, hop right, step left, brush forward right, step right, and close left. The step pattern is *double-hop-step-brush-step-close* (count *4 and 1, 2 and 3 and*).

BUCK TRIPLE TIME STEP

With the weight right, take a double forward left, hop right; double diagonally forward left with left foot, step left, brush right foot forward, step right, and close left to right. Notice that the only difference between this and the single time step is the addition of an extra double step. The step pattern is *double-hop-double-step-brush-step-close* (count *4 and 1 and a 2 and 3 and*).

BREAK STEP

A step that ends a phrase, when it is different from those done throughout the phrase, is a break. It is generally accented and puts a finishing touch on the phrase. It is very characteristically a part of single and triple time routines. Following are examples:

To two waltz time steps starting left, add: step left, swing the right foot forward, hop left, and tap the right toe forward (four measures of 3/4).

To break pattern, do step-swing-hop-tap.

To three single time steps, starting left, double with the right foot, hop left, brush forward right, step right, and close left to right.

Break pattern is double-hop-double-hop-step-lunge.

To three shuffle steps, add two stamps.

Note: These are simple breaks to give you an idea for working. You may substitute anything that suits your fancy and sets the steps off with a punch.

After you have practiced the above basic steps, try your luck at the following practice combinations.

1. Toe-tap eight times with the right foot, describing a half-circle. Repeat with the left.
2. Three doubles right and step right. Repeat left.
3. Double right and step right. Repeat left.
4. Hop left, double right, step right. Repeat left.
5. Shuffle step right, shuffle step left, bells right and left.
6. Two shuffle steps—one right, one left; two bandy turns—one right, one left.
7. Spank right and heel right; spank left and heel left at a walking tempo.
8. Double and ball change left. Repeat on the right.
9. Three buffalo steps and one bell to the left. Repeat to the right.
10. Shuffle step left, shuffle step right, three-step turn left. Repeat, starting right.

Now that you are familiar with the steps, we can talk about dances and *routines,* as they are commonly called. Actually, much of the tap dance we see today is beyond the routine stage of development and is more expressive in movement than merely doing a sequence of steps rhythmically. Traditionally, tap routines are classified into the following types:

Athletic or Acrobatic: A gymnastic sequence combining tap dancing and stunts.

Buck Routine: A tap dance in 2/4 or 4/4 time (foxtrot) which uses the single or triple time buck steps as its foundation. The tempo is fairly fast.

Character: A theme is carried through the routine, expressing something of a rather specific nature, such as characterizing a person or situation.

Military: A dance to a march tune or rhythm in which the style is militaristic.

Soft Shoe: A dance that is characteristically light and covers distance. The tempo is slower than buck time and has a lilting quality. It is graceful in the same sense that a waltz is graceful. *Waltz:* Any dance that is done to waltz or 3/4 time.

Now is the time to have fun making your own routines. Find a tune you like that is not too fast and see what you can put together—or create for yourself. If you pick a waltz, it would be sensible to start with a waltz time step. If you pick a foxtrot, you have a greater range of choice. Listen to the music until you know it so well that you can sing it and feel the phrasing. In foxtrots, most phrasing of popular tunes falls into four or eight repetitions. If you use breaks, they should fall at the end of the phrases. The music you choose should have well-marked rhythm.

Following are some sample routines to help you get started in feeling phrasing. Test yourself on these to see if you can get the rhythm and remember the sequence. For meaning of abbreviations, see pages 30 and 112-114.

SIMPLE SOFT SHOE

Music: Any slow foxtrot, or sing "Way Down upon the Swanee River."

STEPS:
A. Spank R, ball change L-R (1 & 2).
   Repeat to L (3 & 4).
   Bandy turn R (1-4).

   Repeat from beginning, starting L.

B. Grapevine *, starting R (1-4).
   Three step-hops, swing the free leg fwd and describing a small circle
      CW, and stamp L in place without weight (1 & 2 & 3 & 4).

   Repeat, starting L.

C. Shuffle step R, shuffle step L (1 & a 2, 3 & a 4).
   Four prance steps in place, R,L,R,L, placing R foot behind L and L
      behind R. Lean fwd and pick feet up high (1,2,3,4).
   Repeat shuffle step R and L.

D. Spank R, ball-change L-R (1 & 2).
   Repeat to L (3 & 4).
   Bandy turn R (1-4).
   Spank L, ball-change R-L (1 & 2).
   Spank R, ball-change L-R (3 & 4).
   Step L, swing R foot fwd as you hop L.
   Lunge diagonally fwd with arms sdwd (1,2 & 3, hold count 4).

SIMPLE BUCK

Music: Any popular foxtrot tune of moderate tempo.

STEPS:

A. Seven buck single time steps L.
   Break: Double R, hop L, brush R fwd, step R in place, Cl L to R, and
   step fwd R (double-hop-brush-step-close-step).

B. Three Buffalo steps L.
   Leap L in place, leaning bkwd.
   Leap R in front of left, leaning fwd.

   Repeat twice.

   Step-scuff-hop, starting L: step L, scuff R heel as you swing R foot
   fwd, followed by a short hop L. Repeat with R, then L, then R
   again.

C. Hop-double-tap: Hop R, double L diagonally fwd L, tap L behind R.
   Do this four times R, taking weight L on fourth.
   Repeat four times to L.
   Repeat two times R.
   Repeat two times L.
   Repeat once R.
   Repeat once L.
   Repeat once R.
   Repeat once L.

D. Two buck single time steps starting L:
   * Double L, hop R, step L bkwd.
   Double R, hop L, step R bkwd.

   Repeat from *.

   Three buck single time steps.
   Break as in A.

SIMPLE WALTZ TIME

Music: Any waltz of moderate tempo. See suggestions at end of chapter.

A. Four waltz time steps.
   Twelve spank running fwd.
   Four waltz time steps.
   Four step-kick-hops: Step L, swing R across L, and hop L.

B. Three spank steps, traveling diagonally fwd L, and one waltz time
step in place.
Three spank steps traveling diagonally fwd R and one waltz time step
in place.

Repeat the above.

Two waltz time steps in place:
Step in place L, raise R leg diagonally bkwd R, and move bkwd with
two hops (step-hop-hop).

Repeat step-hop-hop R.

Two waltz time steps in place:
Step L, swing R leg fwd scuffing the floor, hop L, slap R foot on
floor fwd.

SELECTED RECORDS FOR TAP DANCING

RCA Victor *Music for Tap Dancing*
(Piano)
LX-1042 *Swingin' Down the Lane*
You Were Meant for Me
Should I
Love Tales
I'm Sitting on Top of the
World
Down Among the Sheltering
Palms
Irene

I'll See you in My Dreams
Three O'Clock in the Morning
When Frances Dances with
Me
Peggy O'Neil
The Man on the Flying Trapeze

Russell Records. P.O. Box 328, Ventura,
California. Catalog available with records
and routines for tap dancing.

SELECTED SOURCES FOR TAP DANCING

Ballwebber, Edith, *Illustrated Tap Rhythms and Routines.* Chicago: Summy, 1933 (out of print).

Duggan, A. S., *The Complete Tap Dance Book.* New York: Ronald Press, 1932.

Fletcher, Beale, *How to Improve Your Tap Dancing.* New York: Ronald Press, 1957.

Frost, Helen, *Tap, Caper and Clog.* New York: Ronald Press, 1932.

Ramsey, Rita, *Home Lessons in Tap Dancing.* New York: E. P. Dutton & Co., Inc., 1932.

Raye, Zilia, *American Tap Dancing.* London: Dancing Times Ltd., 1951.

Sauthoff, Hermine E., *Tap Dance for Fun.* New York: Ronald Press, 1941.

Shipley, Glenn, *Modern Tap Techniques.* San Francisco: Recorder-Sunset Press, 1951.

Sprague, Sidney, *The Sprague "Photovision" Learn to Tap Method.* Englewood, N.J.: Sprague Studies of the Theatre, 1952.

CHAPTER IX

Dance Parties

Dance parties are for fun, and the fun is usually had when you get a group of people together and provide them with things to do that promote the spirit of play. It is important, in planning parties, to think of all the necessities that go into the making of a successful party.

The planning of parties is an absolute necessity if success is to be insured. In her book, *Fun for Parties and Programs*,[1] Catherine Allen organizes the planning of parties into the before, during, and after phases. This book is an inexpensive, well-planned guide that no party lover would be without. Following is a summary of the main points the author makes:

Before people arrive, check to see that—
— The room is clean, attractive, well-ventilated, free from hazards, with the temperature regulated.
— Toilet facilities are available.
— All equipment needed is ready and working; for example, this may include record player, records, pencils, paper, chalk, erasers, whistle, song sheets, seats for tired people, and refreshments arranged.
— Your party program is inclusive and arranged in order.

During the party—
— Start on time.
— Stand where you can be seen and heard.

---

[1] Catherine Allen, *Fun for Parties and Programs.* Englewood Cliffs, N.J.: Prentice-Hall, Inc., 1956, pp. 12-14.

— Get group attention.

— Enjoy what you are doing.

— Get the group organized before you begin activity.

— Teach with confidence.

— Explain directions simply and briefly.

— Teach to the middle of your group.

— Continue an activity as long as people enjoy it.

— Serve refreshments two-thirds of the way through the party.

— Move easily and happily until the end of the evening.

— Close on time with best musical activity.

— Say, "Thank you; good night," and be final.

After the party—think through the evening and evaluate:

— List desirable points.

— List undesirable points.

— Plan for improvement.

Dr. Allen also supplies an excellent score sheet for evaluation through which the individual may diagnose his or her strengths and weaknesses.

Many people take parties for granted; but no party is a success without effective leadership, and this, of course, implies thorough planning, with due consideration for the ages, interests, and abilities of the people who are attending the party.

The beauty of folk dance parties is that people of all ages can take part successfully. In planning the kinds of dances to be included for a party, let your conscience be your guide, but also consider the personal problems confronting the guest.

Folk dances, including square and round, are much more strenuous than social dancing. Clothing worn for an evening of folk dance is comfortable for vigorous activity. This is not true of clothing worn for the social dance mixers. Mixing social dance with an evening of folk dance is possible, although there is no real need for it. However, mixing folk dance with an evening of social dance is enough to cause the party to droop. The guests are not dressed for vigorous activity. Often, the people who come for social dance are not particularly interested in folk dance, and no one should be pressured into doing something he does not want to do at a party. Somehow, the spirit of folk dance and the sophistication of social dance do not mix well. Anyway, each form has enough to offer by itself without supplement from the other form. Many people feel the same way about mixing European folk dance with American square and round.

Be sure to start the evening with some kind of mixer that helps to break the ice and that gets people acquainted. People have fun when they break down barriers between themselves and others. People lose inhibitions very rapidly if the leader is sensitive to the feelings of the group. She must anticipate personal and social insecurities and counteract them by moving the group into activity.

Start with simple activities that everyone can do without deep concentration. Build an element of fun into your activities by adapting materials to your particular group. If partners are a necessity, teach a mixer that will produce partners. However, it is best to start off

J. M. HODGES LIBRARY
WHARTON COUNTY JUNIOR COLLEGE
WHARTON, TEXAS

with an activity that does not require partners.

After the group is moving and feeling more confident, have them do a few dances that are familiar to them and that most people know. Start the dance with a brief review by "walking through" the dance. This will keep many people on the floor who might otherwise be inclined to retire. If all has gone well until now, give your guests a short rest. During this time you might have a novelty event or demonstration or performance of some kind, or some other social activity such as singing or social games.

Following this change of pace, teach the guests new dances. Do it slowly enough to keep your group with you, and be as brief in your explanations as possible. You want to get the dance across as easily as possible and in a relatively short time. Plan your method of presentation before you teach. Teach by building on knowledge that the guests already have. Break down the step patterns into basic steps, and teach them to the music.

Some time during the evening, if not more than once, ask your guests for requests, or have a plan for receiving requests throughout the evening, so that these can be woven into the program in a balanced way that provides an alternation of the more vigorous dances with those that are less tiring.

Refreshments may come next, or light refreshments may be made available between sets of dances, starting about two-thirds of the way through the party and continuing until the end.

Plan a good closing activity that is pleasant and simple for all and yet not exhausting. This should be the kind of dance that leaves the guests in a state of contentment.

Make any announcements that you want guests to remember concerning other parties or events just before the last dance. Announce the last dance as such, and immediately after the dance is over, begin to close shop.

These party plans are, of course, general and adaptable to many situations. The specific adaptation and choice of materials must necessarily be made by you and based on the particular needs of your group. The materials that follow include mixers that are usable for both folk and social dance parties with specific instructions on how to do them. Following this chapter you will find a wealth of excellent source material that will help you plan parties to suit your particular party needs.

Mixers for Folk and Social Dance Parties

HOKEY POKEY   Record: Old Timer 8086

Form a double circle with gents on the inside with their backs to the center. Ladies face partners. Everyone sings the words as they perform the actions. Each repetition moves the group so that everyone has a new partner. The action is the same for everyone. The record listed has calls on one side and no calls on the other, so that you may use it either by having the group sing or by having them follow the call.

Words	*Action*
You put your left hand in,	Place L hand fwd.
You take your left hand out,	Place L hand bkwd.
You put your left hand in,	Place L hand fwd.
And you shake it all about.	Shake L hand.
Now you're doing the Hokey Pokey,	With both hands over head, you turn CW as you move to R to
And you turn yourself around,	meet your new partner.
That's what it's all about, Hey!	Slap knees twice, clap hands once, throw hands over shoulders, and shout "Hey!"

You repeat the above, progressing with following body parts: right hand, left elbow, right elbow, left foot, right foot, left knee, right knee, head, backside, and whole self.

Words	*Action*
At the end, everyone sings, "Hokey Pokey, Hokey Pokey, Hokey Pokey, That's what it's all about, Hey!"	With arms overhead, bow low three times from hips, reaching for the floor with the hands; slap knees twice, clap hands once, throw arms over shoulders, shout "Hey!"

Note: This may also be used in a single circle facing center, without partners, as a means of getting everyone moving.

MIXER FOR SQUARE DANCE   *Record:* Any square dance tune

Gents form an inside circle facing CC, ladies form an outside circle facing CW.

Call	*Action*
Single promenade.	All walk fwd.
Take a partner, circle two.	Men take any lady, join hands, and circle L.
Swing your partner.	Swing partner.
Promenade two by two.	Walk CC with lady on gent's R.
Circle four.	Couples join with another couple and circle L.
Swing your opposite.	Swing the other lady.
Swing your own.	Swing your partner.
Circle eight.	Two couples join with two others and circle L.
Swing your own.	Swing partner.
And there you stand.	End of mixer.

Note: Groups of eight are now organized in four couples ready for a square dance.

OH, SUSANNA [2]

Record: MacGregor 10-762

Form a single circle, a lady on the right of each gent, with everyone facing center. This should be sung by everyone. The dance starts with hands joined in a circle.

Call	Action
Oh, I've come from Alabama with my banjo on my knee,	Everyone walks four steps toward center; all walk bkwd four steps.
And I'm going to Louisiana my true love for to see.	Repeat walks to center, walk bkwd four steps.
It rained all night the day I left,	Ladies go into center four steps.
The weather it was dry,	Ladies walk bkwd four steps.
The sun so hot I froze to death.	Gents go into the circle.
Susanna, don't you cry.	Gents walk bkwd four steps.
Chorus: Oh, Susanna! Don't you cry for me, for I've come from Alabama with my banjo on my knee.	Grand right and left until the end of the chorus; meet a new partner, put her on your R, and circle; then begin again.

GOOFUS MIXER

Record: MacGregor 737

Form a double circle of couples facing CC with a lady on the right of each gent. Partners join inside hands.

Call	Action
Promenade.	Couples walk four steps fwd.
Partners away.	Face partner and back away four steps.
New partners.	Everyone turns ⅛ to own R and walks four steps toward a new partner.
Swing.	Turn partner around once.
Promenade.	Promenade new partner 16 counts.

Note: After the group has moved through the mixer twice and is in time with the music, they will continue without the call.

GRAND MARCH AND ARCH

March: Columbia DX 1246 (*Lancers*) or any spirited march.

The ladies line up on the left side of the room and the gents on the right. Both lines face the front of the room, so that they are walking in the same direction.

---

[2] Catherine Allen, *Fun for Parties and Programs.* Englewood Cliffs, N.J.: Prentice-Hall, Inc., 1956, pp. 46-47.

Call	Action
Forward march.	Both lines walk fwd to end of room.
Down the center by twos.	Each person, as he or she reaches the end of room, turns and walks toward center and joins with partner. They then march down center of room.
Cast off right and left.	First couple goes R, next one L, next one R, and so on, around room again.
Right side arch.	As couples reach head of room and meet, line on R arches as line on L goes under.
Left side arch.	As lines meet again at opposite end of room, other line arches.
Down center by fours.	When lines of couples meet at head of room, two couples join together and come down by fours.
Down the center by eights.	When groups of four meet at head, each joins with another four and comes down eight abreast.

From here you can organize in whatever formation you plan your next activity. If it is a square dance, you have five squares organized. If you want a single circle for games or social activities, break the lines down as they were built up or have the gent at the head group of eight start a single circle by having his group join hands and walk out to his left. The others follow as they reach the front, line two joining with the end of line one, and so on. The leader must spiral the line inside out to get it into one large circle facing center again.

POT LUCK MIXER   *Record:* Polka or Two-Step

Couples are scattered on the floor in open position.

DIRECTIONS: Walk fwd eight steps.
Partners face each other and separate, walking bkwd eight steps.
Turn in any direction and walk fwd eight steps.
Take new partner and two-step in closed position four times.

Social Dance Mixers

MIX AND MATCH   *Record:* Any foxtrot

The men form an inside circle facing CC and the women form another circle facing CW on the outside of the men.

DIRECTIONS: Everyone walks fwd (lines are moving in opposite directions) until the music is stopped.

Each dancer takes the person beside him for a partner, introduces himself, and dances with this partner.

When the music stops, all go back into the circle and repeat.

Once partners are matched, they should be given ample time to dance together before the music is stopped.

CHANGE PARTNERS
Record: Any foxtrot

Couples are scattered on floor, dancing. The leader calls for partners to change. Each couple splits, each person taking a partner near him.

CUT IN

Have a group of five or six men without partners cut in. Anyone without a partner can cut in at any time.

POPULAR SONGS

This is a good mixer for getting the evening started. Slips of paper with popular songs are written in duplicate. As guests arrive, they are given a slip of paper. When the evening activities begin, the guests must go around the room each singing his or her song until two people singing the same song find each other. They are partners for the first dance. You may vary this by matching playing cards, combinations such as salt and pepper, ham and eggs, and so on.

RUM AND TOM COLLINS
Record: Any foxtrot

Couples are scattered on the floor, dancing. The dancers are instructed concerning the meaning of the following cues. They take their cue from the leader, who calls the following:

Rum.   (Continue dancing).
Tom Collins.   (Change partners.)
Rum Collins.   (Stop dead still.)

If dancers move when they are supposed to be still, they are eliminated. The leader who has a good sense of timing can make this a very entertaining game as well as a mixer and contest.

CIRCLE MIXER
Record: Foxtrot or waltz

Have women line up by height (tallest in front) on one side of the room. Have men do the same across the head of the room. The first man takes the first woman and dances her around the room, leaving her at the end of the women's line, the second man takes the second woman, and so forth. As each woman is dropped at the end of the line, the men go forward to get another partner. This is particularly good when there is a shortage of men.

SELECTED RECORDS FOR MIXERS

The following records are suggestions for mixers. In practically all cases, instructions are included with the purchase of records.

Folkraft   1037 *Oklahoma Mixer* (with instructions)
1103 *Skip to My Lou*
1260 *Patty Cake Polka* (calls on one side, instrumental on reverse)
1269 *Red River Valley* (calls on one side, instrumental on reverse)

Lloyd Shaw 121 *Tucker Waltz* (instructions included)
Five Foot Two
117 *Cattle Call Waltz* (instructions included)
Mexican Mixer (instructions included)

Old Timer   8005 *Brown Eyed Mary* (with instructions)
Heel and Toe Polka

SELECTED SOURCES FOR PARTIES

Agricultural Extension Service, *Play Party Games—Sixty Musical Games.* Lafayette, Indiana: Purdue University.

——————, *Socializers for Meetings.* Laramie: The University of Wyoming, College of Agriculture, 1952.

Allen, Catherine L., *Fun for FHA.* Washington, D.C.: Federal Security Agency, 1951.

——————, *Fun for Parties and Programs.* Englewood Cliffs, N.J.: Prentice-Hall, Inc., 1956.

——————, and A. W. Hobt, *Recreation Handbook for Group Leaders.* Knoxville: The University of Tennessee, Division of University Extension, 1946.

Bowers, Ethel, *Parties for Special Days of the Year.* New York: National Recreation Association, 1936.

——————, *Parties, Musical Mixers and Simple Square Dance.* New York: National Recreation Association, 1941.

——————, *Parties Plus: Stunts and Entertainments.* New York: National Recreation Association, 1942.

Geister, Edna, *Ice Breakers and the Ice Breaker Herself.* New York: Harper and Brothers, 1926.

Harbin, E. O., *The Fun Encyclopedia.* Nashville: Cokesbury Press, 1940.

Marsh, Agnes L., and L. P. Marsh, *Textbook of Social Dancing with Complete Plans for Parties.* New York: J. Fischer & Bros., 1933.

Meyer, Harold D., and Charles K. Brightbill, *Community Recreation,* 2nd ed. Englewood Cliffs, N.J.: Prentice-Hall, Inc., 1956.

Rohrbough, Lynn, *Handy II, Kit T, Kit R, Kit P.* Delaware, Ohio: Cooperative Recreation Service.

Sanders, Mary A., *Sing High! Sing Low!* New York: Mary Alison Sanders, 1946.

Also see *Selected Sources* following each of the dance sections in this book.

Glossary

BALL CHANGE—A step pattern in which the weight is taken on the ball of one foot for a very short time and then shifted onto the other foot.

BREAK—In social dancing: A means of separating from partner, or a change from one step to another.

In tap dancing: A change of step with a rhythmic accent at the end of a series of repeated steps. Also, the end of a routine.

CHOREOGRAPHY—The art and craft of composing a dance; the construction and ordering of movement, phrasing, rhythm, design, and dynamics.

COMPOSITION (*See* Choreography.)

CULTURE—The way of life of a group of people, including their observable surface civilization, their social institutions, and their beliefs that form the foundation for their behavior.

DANCE WALK—A basic step pattern in which the transfer of weight is made by sliding the ball of the foot forward and then sinking into the heel of the foot. It is a smooth transference of weight.

DISTORTED MOVEMENT — Movement that takes a form that is unnatural to the body structure.

DRAW STEP—A step pattern in which one foot is brought to the other by pressing the toes against the floor as the close is made.

ELEVATION—Movement that is done above the ground level.

ETHNIC GROUPS—Groups of people who have lived together over a long period of time and developed common ways of living, distinguishable as a culture. The culture can be identified by its beliefs, ideas, values, myths, and traditions.

FOCUS—Concentration of one's thoughts, attention, and movement toward a central point of attraction or activity.

128

GALLOP—A step and leap in an uneven rhythmic pattern. The emphasis is into the air and the push-off is longer than the landing.

GESTURE—A movement symbol that carries a specific meaning. It may be a movement of the head, body, arms, hands, or face. It expresses an idea, attitude, or emotional state.

GRAPEVINE STEP—A step traveling sideward but facing forward made by crossing one leg alternately in back and in front of the other.

IMPROVISATION—The process of creating or composing movement spontaneously in response to a stimulus.

KINESTHESIS—Muscle sense.

LEVEL—The various degrees of height from the floor upward (lying, sitting, kneeling, squatting, standing, jumping).

LOCOMOTION—Traveling from one place to another by using the basic steps, such as the walk, run, hop, leap, jump, or a variation of these steps.

MAZURKA—A step-cut-hop in even rhythm in 3/4 time. Each step gets the same amount of time. The second count is accented.

MOOD—Frame of mind or state of feeling at a particular time.

OPPOSITION HIP SHIFT—The process of separating a step from the shift of weight. When stepping left or forward with the left foot, the hips shift to the right, and vice versa.

PANTOMIME—Movement that describes the action of a person in a particular situation.

PATTER—Rhyme that is inserted to fill dead spaces in a square dance call; also, a style in calling.

PERCUSSIVE MOVEMENT—Movement with a great deal of sudden force, as in striking or exploding; movement that is quick, sharp, and staccato (a great deal of energy released in a small amount of time).

POLKA—Three steps and a hop in an uneven rhythmic pattern in 2/4 time or 6/8 time. The third step is long and the hop is short in time span.

PURE DANCE—Dance composition that has its conception in movement itself and communicates kinesthetically. It does not use any other vehicle for expression, such as drama, gesture, sequence of events, objects, or the like. It is pure movement expression.

ROCK STEP—A step pattern in which the weight is shifted quickly from one foot to the other and occasionally is shifted back and forth many times consecutively.

SCHOTTISCHE—Three steps and a hop in 4/4 time.

SHUFFLE STEP—In square dance: A walking step in which the dancer lightly slides the feet along the floor.
In tap dance: A step pattern made up of a double, a hop, and a skip.

SINGING CALL—A square dance call that is sung to a specific tune.

SKIP—A step and a hop in an uneven rhythmic pattern in 2/4 or 6/8 time. The step is longer than the hop.

SLIDE—A step close in an uneven rhythmic pattern in which the feet stay close to the floor. The emphasis is into the floor, and the step is longer than the leap in time span.

SPACE AWARENESS — Awareness of one's movement in relation to spatial forces.

SPONTANEITY—The quality of responding or acting from impulse; action without planning.

SUSTAINED MOVEMENT—Movement in which the action is carried on for a long period of time; movement in which the release of energy is steady and continuous.

SWINGING MOVEMENT — Movement that passes through the lower half of an arc and is forceful at the beginning, has an element of momentum, and a point of suspension at the end of the arc.

SYNCOPATION—The act of accenting the usually unaccented beats of a measure. Emphasis on the off-beat, such as count 2 & 4 as opposed to 1 & 3.

THEME AND VARIATION—Statement of an idea in movement followed by any number of variations on the original statement.

TWO-STEP—A step-close-step in 2/4 or 4/4 time.

VARIATION—Transformation of a theme; deviation of movement from a set theme or norm; change in condition, character, or degree.

VIBRATORY MOVEMENT—Movement that is small and very fast, such as is observed in shivering.

WALTZ—A step-step-close in 3/4 time.

Dance Periodicals

American Squares, 1159 Broad Street, Newark 5, N.J.

Dance Magazine, 231 W. 58th St., New York, N.Y.

Dance News, 119 West 57th St., New York, N.Y.

Dance Observer, Box 473, Madison Square Station, New York 3, N.Y.

Foot and Fiddle, Box 268, Ruidoso, New Mexico.

Foot Notes, 1957 P.O. Box 267, South Tacoma 9, Washington.

Let's Dance, 150 Powell Street, Room 302, San Francisco 2, Calif.

Sets in Order, 462 N. Robertson Blvd., Los Angeles 48, Calif.

The Folk Dancer, P.O. Box 201, Flushing, N.Y.

The Folk Lorist, 505 Wilbraham Road, Manchester 21, England.

Record Dealers

Deibel, Inc., 1465 Hodiamont Ave., St. Louis 12, Missouri. Carries all labels.

Ed Kremer's Record Shop, 262 O'Farrell Street, No. 301, United Nations Theatre Bldg., San Francisco, Calif.

Educational Dance Recordings, Inc., P.O. Box 6062, Bridgeport 6, Conn. Records for social dancing, Foxtrot, Mambo, Rhumba, Waltz, Samba, Tango, and others.

Folkraft, 1159 Broad Street, Newark 5, N.J. Complete line of folk records.

Folk Dance Federation of California, 262 O'Farrell Street, San Francisco 2, Calif. Records and descriptions for a broad range of folk dances.

Folkways Record and Service Corp., 117 West 46th St., New York 19, N.Y.

Harry Berliner's Music Shop, 154 Fourth Avenue, New York 3, N.Y. Complete line of all labels for folk dancing.

Johnson Brothers Record Shop, 5512 20th St., N.W., Seattle, Washington.

Lloyd Shaw Recordings, Box 203, Colorado Springs, Colorado. Carries Lloyd Shaw recordings only.

Methodist Records, 810 Broadway, Nashville, Tennessee. Carries World of Fun Series only.

Michael Herman Folk Dance Records, Box 201, Flushing, N.Y. Carries a broad range of folk dance records with descriptions.

Morry's Folk Dance Record Shop, 703 Hennepin, Minneapolis, Minnesota. Carries all labels for folk dance.

Russell Records, P.O. Box 328, Ventura, Calif. Records for all types of dancing.

Sam Goody Records, 235 West 49th St., New York 19, N.Y. Carries records of all labels.

Sets in Order, Square Dance Square, Summerland, Calif.

The Folklore Center, 4100 University Way, Seattle, Washington.

Western Jubilee Master Record Service, 708 E. Garfield, Phoenix, Arizona.

Record Companies

ASP Record Co., 1779 S. Crescent Heights Blvd., Los Angeles, Calif.

Black Mountain Records, 1732 Stanton Avenue, Glendale, Calif.

Capitol Record Company, Sunset and Vine, Hollywood, Calif.

Columbia Record Company, 1473 Burnum Avenue, Bridgeport, Conn.

Decca Record Company, 50 West 57th St., New York 17, N.Y.

Folk Dancer Record Service, P.O. Box 201, Flushing, N.Y.

Imperial Records, 137 North Western Avenue, Los Angeles 4, Calif.

Kismet Record Company, 227 East 14th St., New York 3, N.Y.

Linden Records, Inc., 2417 Second Avenue, Seattle, Washington.

MacGregor Company, 729 Western Avenue, Hollywod 5, Calif.

Methodist Publishing House, Audio-visual Dept., 810 Broadway, Nashville, Tennessee.

Old Timer Records, 370 N. 7th Street, Phoenix, Arizona.

Radio Corporation of America, Educational Service, Camden, N.J.

Sonart Record Company, 251 West 42nd St., New York 18, N.Y.

Windsor Record Company, 5528 N. Rosemead Blvd., Temple City, Calif.

Index

12769
2950 041